D1462142

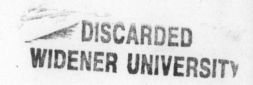

REFLECTIONS ON THE CONSTITUTION

REFLECTIONS

ON THE

CONSTITUTION

THE HOUSE OF COMMONS
THE CABINET
THE CIVIL SERVICE

by

HAROLD J. LASKI

MANCHESTER UNIVERSITY PRESS

© 1951
Published by the University of Manchester at
THE UNIVERSITY PRESS
316–324, Oxford Road, Manchester, 13

First Published 1951
Fourth Printing 1962

Printed in Great Britain by Butler & Tanner Ltd., Frome and London

PREFATORY NOTE

THE late Professor Laski was invited to deliver three public lectures in the University of Manchester in February 1950. He gave these lectures to large audiences in the week beginning 6th February: for the next fortnight he was actively engaged in the General Election, which was decided on 23rd February; and on 25th March he died. The text of the lectures as it stands is stamped with his personality, and even with the accent and manner of his delivery, but it lacks his final revision. It is impossible to guess what changes he would have made: some corrections have been necessary before publication, but these have been limited to minor points of fact and grammar, and to the insertion of section headings.

58111

CONTENTS

PART ONE

THE HOUSE OF COMMONS

CONTEMPORARY CRITICISMS OF PARLIAMENT

IT is an exceptional pleasure to me to have been invited to give these lectures in the University of Manchester. It is not merely that I am myself Manchester born and Manchester bred. I owe much to the inspiration I received from men whose names are household words in this university—from Samuel Alexander, from T. F. Tout, and from Michael Sadler among its teachers, from C. P. Scott among the citizens of Manchester, who, in my youth, thought the status of this university a matter of immense importance to the quality of its civic life, and to my friend, Lord Simon of Wythenshawe, who, with Lady Simon, has, if I may say so, given to this city a continuity of devoted service not less important than the generosity he has shown it. I come to the University of Manchester from an institution which, if younger than yours, has had the good fortune to have its traditions established and given shape by one who thought, as the men who developed the University of Manchester thought, that the first task of learning and scholarship is not research for its own sake, but the achievement of a profounder knowledge of men's relation to nature. They were, I think rightly, convinced that there was no other way in which to discover the questions we should ask in the hope of transforming Man from a rebel against a harsh and unfriendly universe into a master of its forces, and thus into that self-mastery that is one of the essential conditions of a free society.

Our age is one of turbulence and confusion, in which the large-scale breakdown of traditional values has made many doubt the validity even of the institutions which lie at the basis of our national life. I propose, therefore, in these lectures, to re-examine two great institutions, confidence in which is the obvious clue to the maintenance of a democratic society. I propose to examine the present condition of the House of Commons, and that of the Cabinet, and, in part, of the Civil Service, upon the efficiency and imaginative capacity of which so much of the adequacy of Parliamentary government depends. I do not need to tell you that, especially in the last thirty years, there has been a growing suspicion, both on the Right and on the Left, about their adequacy in relation to the immense problems we have to solve. Severe judgments have been passed upon the effectiveness of the House of Commons not only by those who have observed it merely from without, but, hardly less, by many who have known it intimately from within. We have been asked to regard it as nothing but an organ of registration for the Cabinet, a body of miscellaneous amateurs, whose discussions do not count, whose criticism and investigations go unheeded, whose independence has been so impaired by the rigidity of party discipline that it has lost the high status it once enjoyed when the whole nation watched with passionate interest the epic contests in which men like Gladstone and Disraeli crossed swords in debate. We have been told that it has delegated so much of its power to Ministers and the officials of their Departments that it can no longer protect the freedom of citizens nor safeguard their property from the inexhaustible rapacity of a ruthless bureaucracy. We are urged to regard it as in need of reforms so massive that when it emerged from their acceptance it would no longer be recognisable as the classic institution to which so many admiring tributes were wont to be paid. Nor, indeed, has the Cabinet been spared by the critics. Its influence has diminished, in the first place, as the power of the Prime Minister has grown. Perhaps no more than a quarter of its members are really influential; they constitute an inner oligarchy which has reduced the rest to a body of pale ghosts who are only less surprised at the formal eminence for which they have been selected than are their friends at the fact of their choice. In any case, it has been urged, the work of most Government Departments is now so massive and so exacting that only a Minister, not only of exceptional power, but also of outstanding character, can really operate his own office in terms of a policy that is his own; the real truth is that most of them are, in the hands of their officials, little more than puppets who dance on wires the movement of which is controlled by a small number of civil servants who have exchanged the trappings of formal dignity for the reality of effective power. It is, moreover, rare in these days for a Minister to know his Department well enough when he arrives there for the first time genuinely to be able to take charge of its activities. The alternative to trusting his officials to show him the way is to make mistakes of such proportions as to make him an obvious liability to the Government whom the Prime Minister will quickly change for someone who achieves the reputation of being an asset. But to be an asset, the critics insist, either the Minister must be seen and not heard or he must place himself in the hands of his officials who will guide him to some small achievement and prevent him from making mistakes. The remarkable politician apart, a dutiful obedience to the administrative heads of his Department is much the most direct road to the reputation of a sound and knowledgeable man.

But we are sternly admonished against the danger of confidence in the bureaucracy. The little officials, generally speaking, are not only greedy for power, they have a habit of strangling themselves in their own red tape. They compose complicated regulations in a style no one, not even themselves, can understand. They do everything with painful slowness, and with a relentless search for the routine of uniformity. They lack the initiative and the directness of business men. They make irritating rules which interfere, as in industry and commerce, with practical affairs of which they have no first-hand experience. They make, only too often, a "theoretical" approach to a problem laid before them. They insist on a vast expenditure of man-power in filling out innumerable forms which consume the time and energy clearly capable of being spent to much better purpose. They are always investigating, peeping and prying into other people's business, compelling submission to rules and orders which prevent their victims from getting on with their work.

They hamper freedom, by controlling this and rationing that, and limiting what a business man can do with his own profit. Since most of them have had a training, not in the hard school of life, but in classics or history, mathematics or philosophy, they always approach the issues upon which they have to pass judgment with the mind of a doctrinaire, remote from the real world where men rely upon each other's word, and there is little need for the irritating ways which make them insist on putting everything down on paper. There are always far too many of them, generally doing too little work; if a company were run as they run a Department, it would rush headlong into bankruptcy. They have no incentive to take risks, with the result that their caution infuriates the enterprising and audacious merchant adventurers who, when they were left alone, laid the foundation of this country's greatness. Only those who have had dealings with the Civil Service can appreciate that the famous maxim *ne trop pas gouverner* has the status of a natural law. They become fixed, at an early stage of life, in a traditional way of doing things, so that their habits fail to get adjusted to the ever-changing pattern of the outside world.

II

PARLIAMENTARY GOVERNMENT IN THE TWENTIETH CENTURY

No one would seriously suggest that the House of Commons should refuse to permit the adaptation of its habits

to the new demands of a civilisation that has probably
changed more intensely, since 1906, than it had done in
the 218 years from the "glorious Revolution", and the
famous Liberal victory, though itself perhaps the final
symbol of the end of the Victorian age, seems, even to
people who remember it as vividly as I do, almost an
infinite distance away. In 1906, we were far from universal suffrage. The whole of the national expenditure
was little more than a quarter of what today we spend on
defence alone. We had immense foreign investments, and
Mr. Chamberlain's campaign for a protective tariff had
foundered upon what seemed the impregnable rock of
the national faith in free trade. The Labour Party had
only 29 members in the House of Commons, and a careful foreign observer was about to predict that it was
destined to remain little more than an influential wing of
the Liberal Party. It was hardly a year since the careful
efforts of the Foreign Office had transformed our bad relations with France into that *Entente Cordiale* which
would, it was hoped, maintain a balance of power strong
enough to dissuade the Germany of Wilhelm from seeking to realise undue ambitions in trade and colonial expansion. There were no Ministries of Defence or Health,
of Labour or Transport or Supply. The possession of a
private income of £400 per annum was, and remained
until 1919, a necessary condition of entrance into the Diplomatic Service. It was only four years since an eminent
peer had been Prime Minister, and although Sir Henry
Campbell-Bannerman resisted the effort of Sir Edward
Grey to force him into the House of Lords, neither man
regarded membership of the Upper House as an obstacle

to holding that office; no one dreamed in 1906 that Lord Salisbury would pretty certainly prove to have been the last peer to become Prime Minister. There was no such conception as Dominion Status; the foreign policy of those nations which are now our equal partners in the Commonwealth was carried out, on their behalf, by the Foreign Secretary in London. India was still governed much as it had been after the transfer of power from John Company to the Crown in 1858; and, as late as 1909, Edward VII was deeply dissatisfied with Lord Morley's proposal to have an Indian member of the Secretary of State's Council in London. The Irish members still sat at Westminster; and parties watched uneasily the exercise of power by John Redmond and his supporters without doubting for one moment that, Ulster apart, they had unquestionable authority to speak for the rest of Ireland. There was no health insurance, no unemployment pay; apart from Mr. and Mrs. Webb, and that young leader-writer on the *Morning Post*, now Lord Beveridge, I doubt whether anyone, least of all Mr. Churchill, had ever heard of a Labour Exchange. It is not, I think, an exaggeration to say that, in 1906, not six members of the Labour Party had ever heard of Lenin, and no one in this country had any grasp of the significance of that famous Conference in the Brotherhood Chapel in Southgate Road which created the Bolshevik Party. Nor must we forget that in 1906 members of Parliament were not paid; and it was not until 1909 that the Law Lords, in the notorious *Osborne* case, decided, on grounds of "public policy", that it was *ultra vires* for a trade union to raise a political fund from such of their members as did not "contract out" of that obligation, through which they were able to pay a modest competence to their representatives in the House of Commons. Not the least eloquent or interesting speech upon the Bill which overrode the decision of the Law Lords was the one made by Mr. Winston Churchill, in which he explained his full sympathy with the trade unions' suspicion that the Courts of Justice were biased against Labour organisations.

We are told by so experienced an observer as Mr. Amery that Parliamentary government is already dead, and has been replaced by Cabinet government. The critics tell us that, despite the wider social range from which members of the House of Commons are now drawn, compared, say, with the year 1832, the member of Parliament today is less able, less independent, and far less competent to form an opinion upon the matters upon which he votes than was his predecessor. Our attention is drawn to the fact that nearly all important legislation is government legislation and that those private members are few indeed who can hope to pilot a Bill of their own to the statute-book. Debates, it is argued, have become mere formalities, tolerated by the Government only because they do not affect the result in the division lobby. Far too many Bills are passed, and far too few of them are debated with sufficient amplitude. Too many are sent upstairs to have their details settled in one of the Committees which now deal with all but the most vital legislation. There are bitter criticisms of the growth of delegated legislation, and of the consequential growth of administrative law —a growth predicted more than sixty years ago by Maitland—and it is insisted that the rule of Law and the freedom of the citizen are gravely menaced by these developments. Some argue that the House of Commons sits for too many months in the year. Mr. Christopher Hollis has recently complained not only that it is useless to raise matters of debate on the adjournment, but even that question time is less significant than it used to be, and that, "a great deal more often than not", it is far easier to get a constituent's grievance remedied by a private letter to the Department concerned than to raise it in the House, where the reluctance of a Minister and his officials to admit a mistake in public gets them on their dignity and makes them adamant rather than open-minded and rational. Many critics are irritated by the fact that Ministers refuse to answer questions on the day-to-day decisions taken by the Boards of nationalised industries. Others complain that the hours during which the House sits are far too long, and that the frequency of all-night sittings is indefensible. If we add up all the complaints, and accept them at the face value they are given by those who put them forward, it would almost seem as though one might as well get rid of the House of Commons altogether. Yet I think that most of the critics whose good-will is not in doubt would, if pressed, admit the real alternative to the House of Commons is the concentration camp. Where a legislative assembly goes on discussing its business in the certain knowledge that in not more than five years from the first day of its first session it will have to submit its work to the free judgment of what is, I think, by far the most mature electorate in the world, I think there is real ground for saying that discussion does matter very seriously, and that the critics

B

have set most of their complaints in a distorted historical perspective.

Let me begin with the incisive attack of Mr. Amery, perhaps the most distinguished of the critics, and certainly the one with the longest first-hand experience of the issues he discusses. He begins with a complaint against Bagehot for arguing in his *English Constitution* that the system under which we are governed is Parliamentary government. That is not so, Mr. Amery emphasises; we are governed by the Cabinet and not by Parliament; Bagehot mistook the real source of effective power. With great respect to Mr. Amery his strictures are gravely unjust to Bagehot. The central theme of Bagehot's remarkable book consists of a brilliant exploration of his famous discovery that the Cabinet is the "hyphen that joins, the buckle that links" the executive power of the Government to its legislative power. That Bagehot attached much more importance to the House of Commons as a body of members less organised and disciplined than they are today is due to the fact that the first edition of his book was published before the Reform Act of 1867, even more, before that government of Mr. Gladstone in 1868 which may really be said to have given the two-party system in its present form something like its letters of credit. I venture the guess that, when he wrote, more private members had an individual importance than they have today; but I think the reason for their importance was not the lesser importance of the Cabinet, but the fact that more members of Parliament represented a select and even jealous oligarchy, hostile to those who came from outside their ranks, and far more eager to insist that the

House of Commons confined its attention to the narrowest possible area of action, than was to prove possible after the overwhelming changes in the character of our lives since 1906, still more since 1919, and above all since 1945.

Let us look at this statistically. The Whig Liberal Party of 1865, elected, probably, while Bagehot was writing, had 195 members who represented the land-holding interest, and 51 who were by profession soldiers and sailors; the comparative figures for the Tory Party were 199 and 65. The differences between these figures are not very striking; but, in 1865 in the Whig Liberal Party there were over 350 members who, though they might be landowners as well, had a stake also in finance and industry, while in the Tory Party, on the same basis, finance and industry accounted only for 136. In 1865 there were 58 lawyers in the Whig Liberal Party; in the Tory Party there were only 25. Among the Radicals in the House in 1832, 18 land-owners formed the single largest group; there was no land-owner among the Radicals in 1865. Or if we take those who stood for the repeal of the Act of Union with Ireland in 1832, 27 out of 51 were landowners; in 1865, out of 15 supporters in the House, repeal had only two land-owners among its supporters. If we take Mr. Gladstone's party in 1868, he was supported by 197 land-owners, much the largest group; the Conservative Party had only 150; in the House of Commons of 1900, there were only 30 land-owners in the Liberal Party as against 150 land-owners in the Conservative Party—a larger number than at any time since Disraeli's famous victory of 1874; while between the elections of 1868 and

1900, the land-owners among the Radicals varied between a minimum of none in 1868 and 1874 and a maximum of four in 1892, which dwindled to three in each of the two Parliaments of 1895 and 1900.

It is clear, in short, that at least up to the Reform Act of 1867 the House of Commons mainly conceived itself as a body the purpose of which was to safeguard property against the danger of numbers; in the debates on that Act Disraeli made it clear that he regarded democracy as a "thoroughly vicious form of government", and that the Government believed strongly in the need to maintain the authority of property-owners under the constitution. It is difficult, until Mr. Gladstone's Government of 1868, not to regard the House of Commons as essentially a body of property-owners—the Tories desiring to safeguard the interest of the land and the Whigs and the Liberals the interests of commerce and industry. Both sides strongly favoured a policy of *laissez-faire*; and despite collectivist legislation like the Factory Acts, the doctrine that the Government should interfere with the life of the individual was the exception, and not the rule, in legislation. It is not really excessive to say that, up to 1868, there was practical agreement on both sides of the House that the "British people" was composed of the nobility, the country gentry, and the middle classes, and that below them there was "the mob" which did not count. One can see in the speeches of Brougham and Macaulay, as in the writings of James Mill, not only the ardent acceptance of the "stake in the country" argument but the fear that admission of those citizens without a stake in the country would endanger the very foundations of property itself.

That was why Macaulay devoted all his rhetorical powers to denouncing the Chartist Petition; and it is interesting to note that for something like fifteen years after the failure of Chartism, there were few citizens among the working class, not belonging to a skilled craft, who relied upon either political or industrial action to rescue them from their hopelessness about the future in a community which, private charity to those termed the "respectable poor" apart, had but a faint interest in their welfare.

I suggest, therefore, that one reason why, before 1868, the House of Commons seems a leisured assembly, the members of which are not tied with any rigidity to party discipline, is that the government rarely devoted its attention to those members of the community who most required it. Little time is spent on education before the Act of 1870; no time is spent on housing or on unemployment or on industrial organisation; public health only occupied members with any continuity after the Disraeli Government of 1874. After 1868 the situation begins to change. Mr. Forster put the Education Act of 1870 on the statute-book. The trade unions began to be a pressure-group of considerable power; and their legal right to conditions under which they could effectively organise became a matter of deep Parliamentary significance. When Mr. Gladstone sponsored the disestablishment of the Irish Church in 1869 he opened up a great range of questions it was impossible for the House of Commons to evade; and the Irish Nationalists, under the leadership of Parnell, raised the practice of obstruction to the level of a fine art. The Irish Land Act of 1870, a fiercely contested

Act, occupied twenty-five days of Parliamentary time in the House of Commons; that of 1881 occupied fifty-eight. Those who speak of the "absurd hours" for which the Commons now sit, the excessive burden of all-night sittings, might well reflect upon Lord Morley's comment upon the price of the Irish question in Mr. Gladstone's Government of 1880. "The House of Commons", he has written,[1] "sat for one hundred and fifty-four days and for 1400 hours; some 240 of these hours were after midnight. Only three times since the Reform Bill had the House sat for more days; only once, in 1847, had the total number of hours been exceeded and that only by seven, and never before had the House sat so many hours after midnight."

The truth thus seems to be a relatively simple one. As Great Britain was transformed from a mainly agricultural to a predominantly industrial state, ever more complex problems of organising so different a community emerged. Urban development in the rapidly growing towns, the growth of railways, the new dimension in which the public health had to be regarded, the call of industrialism for literacy, the resolute effort of the workers to combine for their own protection, the correlation between economic misery, nationalism and violence in Ireland, gave rise to problems which all serious observers saw could only be solved by government intervention. Once there was the need for government intervention, each party required a programme to explain the extent and character of the intervention it would attempt, if it were given a majority by the electorate. But the search

[1] *Life of Gladstone*, Vol. II, p. 222.

for a majority required effective organisation of the party
in the constituencies, and effective discipline of its members inside the House of Commons; the latter became
exceptionally urgent when Parnell used Parliamentary
obstruction as a technique of obstruction in the 'seventies,
and Lord Randolph Churchill and his "Fourth Party"
adapted it to their special requirements in the 'eighties.
Once party organisation in the electorate became necessary on a national level, each party encountered doctrinal
tendencies and pressures of interest, of which Mr. Joseph
Chamberlain and his followers, especially that remarkable
party official, Mr. Schnadhorst, took full advantage by
inventing procedures of which the original purpose was
to transform a Liberal Party in which Whig ideas had
overwhelming authority, to one in which Radical ideas
had the upper hand. Lord Randolph Churchill was quick
to see the importance of Mr. Chamberlain's discovery for
the Tory Party, and he sought to adapt it, under the
patronage of Disraeli's great name, to make an appeal to
the working-class voter to think of Toryism as democratic, instead of being a combination of reactionary land-
owners, Nonconformist-hating Anglican parsons, and
members of the professions, chiefly legal, who looked
upon the House of Commons as a sure road to social promotion and, in the case of lawyers, elevation to the
Bench as the final fulfilment of the carpet-bagger's career.

Irish Home Rule apart, this really meant that, from
1832 until 1924, the two parties between which the power
to govern was divided differed only in the emphasis they
gave to one or another of a common body of principles;
it was almost an axiom of both that they agreed not to go

outside the common body of principles they shared. Important as were their differences upon Ireland, they were never so divided upon them that, before 1912, social peace was threatened. And that threat, in its turn, did not stand by itself, but was closely correlated with the rapid rise, after 1906, of the Labour Party, which drove the Liberals into far-reaching social measures lest the reliance which the leadership of Mr. Gladstone had enabled them to place upon a fairly solid working-class support should break down. But the price the Liberal Government of Mr. Asquith had to pay for getting its social measures passed by Parliament was a direct attack upon the powers of the House of Lords, itself the source of the ultimate power of past traditions to regulate the pace of change. The measures themselves seemed much too radical for the Tory leaders in any case; and important limitations upon freedom of debate were necessary even to drive them through the House of Commons. The new legislation, the new procedure, and the important limitation upon the powers of the Lords, all seemed to combine to open an abyss between Liberals and Tories which many of them contemplated with a good deal of dismay. That was why, in 1910, there were the confidential discussions made with the knowledge of the then Prime Minister, Mr. Asquith, in which Mr. Lloyd George put forward by means of a letter to Mr. Balfour, the idea of a Coalition Government.[1]

To the understanding of our contemporary situation, some phrases in Mr. Lloyd George's letter are of outstand-

[1] Charles Petrie, *Life and Letters of Austen Chamberlain* (London 1939), pp. 257 ff. The full text of Mr. Lloyd George's letter is given at pp. 381 f.

ing importance. "Some of the urgent problems awaiting settlement," he wrote to Balfour, "problems which concern intimately the happiness and the efficiency of the inhabitants of these islands, their strength and influence, can only be successfully coped with by the active co-operation of both the great Parties in the State. Parties will always disagree on certain vital issues affecting the government of the country; their respective points of view are essentially different; but at the present moment the questions which are of the most vital importance to the well-being of the great community are all questions which are not only capable of being settled by the joint action of the two great Parties without involving any sacrifice of principle on the part of either, but which can be better served by such co-operation than by the normal working of Party machinery. This country has gained a good deal from the rivalry and conflict of Parties, and it will gain a good deal more in the future from the same cause; but I cannot help thinking that the time has arrived for a truce, for bringing the resources of the two Parties into joint stock, in order to liquidate arrears which, if much longer neglected, may end in national impoverishment, if not insolvency." Mr. Lloyd George then suggested that coalition was necessary in order to mobilise the resources of Great Britain and its Empire against the strain of foreign competition. If a Coalition could be formed, he thought it would be able to solve the housing problem, the drink problem, national insurance against ill-health, sudden death, old age and unemployment. It could overhaul the Poor Law, re-organise and develop education, especially on the technical side, and reform the structure of local government. He thought that a much larger provision could be made for national defence. He was in favour of examining the problems connected with Government assistance to trade and commerce and looking at the problems of tariffs and inland transport from a more intelligent angle. He was anxious to secure acceptance of large-scale farming "by competent persons with adequate capital". He felt that a Coalition might achieve greater imperial unity and a far better use of joint resources both for defence and commerce. Finally, he suggested that since such a Government would represent the whole nation, its creation "would undoubtedly enhance the prestige of this country abroad".

Mr. Lloyd George's scheme failed after some conferences between leading men on both sides, and even a provisional allocation of offices to some, at least, of the party-leaders. Its interest is twofold. It partly embodies, in the first place, the purposes Mr. Lloyd George himself sought to fulfil in the six years of his Premiership in a Coalition Government, as well as the proof that the sacrifices its fulfilment would have called for were judged unacceptable to either side by its leaders, even when they were called for in the dramatic circumstances of war; and though it is known that, in 1910, Mr. Lloyd George consulted Mr. Ramsay MacDonald in a private capacity on his scheme, he did not think it necessary to assume that the Labour Party should be officially included in the ambit of his proposals. Obviously, in his view, the rivalry of Liberal and Tory could always be transcended by a Coalition which would emphasise, in a critical situation, how wide was the area of their common agreement. In

1910, he either did not regard the Labour Party as an organisation with an important future, or he took the view that it had objectives which would render the membership of such a Government inconsistent with a unity of any duration.

Up to the outbreak of the first World War in 1914, it is not very far from the truth to say that we were governed by a single party divided into two groups each of which had little difficulty in accepting the same major principles of action. There were difficulties about minor matters, no doubt; and there was a sense, growingly vivid after 1906, that the entry of the Labour Party on to the scene would compel some adjustment of those major principles. No one can look at the attitude of the Tories to the Trades Disputes Act of 1906 or the Trade Union Act of 1913 without realising their resentment at the political implications of working-class organisation and method; and, in much the same way, I think the Liberal view of that legislation is less a direct welcome to it than a recognition that only by sponsoring it could a permanent split in the half-acknowledged alliance between the Liberal and Labour Parties be avoided. If it be said that Liberals and Tories were deeply divided both on Ireland and the House of Lords, I think the answer is that this was not really the case. On Ireland, the real division was on the question of how far Ulster was entitled to exceptional treatment, and on this issue Mr. Lloyd George and Mr. Churchill shared most of the Tory outlook, though their tactical approach was different, and Sir Austen Chamberlain and Lord Birkenhead were to help them to put it into law in 1921. On the House of Lords, the main figures in both parties agreed that the financial supremacy of the Commons must be maintained; on the Lords' powers on other questions they differed, I suggest, less in kind than in degree. The Tories' approach seemed far more different than it was for two reasons. First, they favoured a much slower rate of change than Liberals who knew that their hold on office depended upon their ability to keep the support of the Irish and the Labour members; and, second, Lord Lansdowne, the Tory leader in the Lords, was swept on one side by the "backwoodsmen" who were prepared, on this occasion, to safeguard the last bastions of their privileged position very much on the ground that once they gave up a part, they ceased to be able, on some future occasion, to defend the rest. Their anxiety, like that of the late Lord Salisbury, was, even at the risk of constitutional explosion, to remain an ultimate reserve power in the state, which could always prevent the passage of what they regarded as "dangerous" legislation. They wanted to keep the historic proportions of influence between classes in church and state permanently unchanged; and an examination of their speeches, made in despite of their leaders, shows, I think, that their next real anxiety was to prevent drastic social, not to say socialist, legislation being enacted through the forms of a constitution the spirit of which they regarded as out of accord with purposes of this kind.

The "backwoodsmen" were, no doubt, extremists; but if one remembers two of the outstanding results of the first World War, it is clear that they saw further than perhaps they knew. For, on the one hand, the "coupon" election of 1918 was the beginning of that swift decline

from which the Liberal Party has not been able to recover; from 1922 onwards, the Labour Party has always
been either the official Opposition or the Government.
On the other hand, the main preoccupation of the House
of Commons since 1918 has been with economic and
social problems, the close analysis of which has made it
increasingly evident that our basic ideas of property and
the valid sphere of Government action are undergoing
changes as fundamental as those which were made after
the Civil Wars in the seventeenth century, and after the
Reform Bill of 1832 in the nineteenth.

It is the fact that the Labour Party has become the alternative Government to the Conservative Party which has
altered so profoundly the character of Parliament, and its
relation to the Cabinet and the Civil Service in the last
thirty years. That can, I suggest, be seen in many different
ways. Broadly speaking, the sources from which Conservative members of the House of Commons are drawn
have not changed very much since 1868; but the sources
from which the Labour Party draws its members are very
different from those of the old Liberal Party. For one
thing, most of the old Whig families are now solidly
ensconced in the Conservative Party; for another, I think
I am right in saying that no trade unionist has ever been a
Conservative member of Parliament. If one examines the
composition of the Conservative Party in the House of
Commons its members are heirs to peerages, members of
the old families, bankers and financiers, lawyers and
business men, with a scattering of teachers, retired soldiers
and sailors, a few doctors, a few journalists and so forth.
Mr. Churchill, in fact, leads a party the elements in which

are not very different from those which composed it when Lord Salisbury was its leader almost half a century ago; and, looking at the Front Opposition Bench, it does not appear obvious that he would form a Cabinet markedly different from that led by Lord Salisbury. The contrast with the Labour Party is striking. About half the Labour Party is, as a rule, composed of ex-officials of trade unions or of men engaged in manual work and members of a union for an important part of their lives; and in Mr. Attlee's Cabinet today five posts are held by ex-officials of trade unions, and one by a leading ex-official of the Co-operative Movement. Though it is, of course, true, that the external world both parties have to consider is the same world, each of them, whether as Government or as Opposition, is likely to approach the problems of that external world from an angle which weights them a good deal differently because the character of the experience represented in each of the parties makes its members see them in a very different perspective. Take only the single issue of the relation of the trade unions to politics—what even so subtle a Tory democrat as Mr. R. A. Butler calls "setting the trade unions free from dependence upon a political party" obviously appears to Mr. Ernest Bevin an indefensible effort to fasten new chains upon them. One has but to read the forcible and angry speech he made in 1946 in support of the repeal of the Trade Disputes and Trade Unions Act of 1927 to realise that his conception of trade union "freedom" has no relation at all to the considerations which govern Mr. Butler's approach to that same issue.

The nature and volume of the problems to be discussed

by the contemporary House of Commons, moreover, makes the character of its debates quite different from anything generally regarded as normal even before 1914. Political problems in the classic sense of the term, the franchise, the place of the church in the nation's life, temperance reform, Irish Home Rule, the powers of the House of Lords, were all matters it was easier to discuss in a general way that was interesting not only to the general public, but also to members themselves, than many of the highly technical issues upon which the House of Commons has now to make up its mind. There is no difficulty that I have been able to discover in arousing deep interest in any large matter of general principle. There is no difficulty, either, in arousing deep interest in any matter that is the centre of crisis, internal or external; a vote of censure upon the Government, for example, will always arouse an unmistakable interest. But it is hardly to be expected that the details of a Derating Act when, as a Bill, it is in the Committee stage, or the exact forms in which authority will be devolved in an Education Act, for example, upon a Part III authority, will make the electorate as interested as a discussion of the wisdom or unwisdom of the Government's action in deciding to devalue the pound sterling in relation to the dollar by about one-third.

I have read with great care the criticisms of contemporary Parliaments in relation to the past, as well as the proposals for making the Parliament of today more efficient in relation to its business. I must confess to doubts whether the criticisms are valid, and, with an important exception that I shall note presently, I am bound to say that most of the proposals which aim at greater efficiency seem to me to be ill-conceived for this purpose. In 1931, for example, Sir Austen Chamberlain told the Select Committee on Procedure in the Public Business that he did not think the reputation of the House stood as high as when he first entered it over forty years before, and that the quality of the speaking was nothing like so good. Other members complained to the Select Committee that the rights of private members were being invaded, that the House did not sufficiently control the Executive, especially in matters of national expenditure, and that debates were not as interesting as they used to be. A close examination of Sir Austen's evidence, and of that of those who thought with him, seems to amount to three points. The first is that, apart from *The Times* and a small number of other journals, the debates in the House are less adequately reported than in the 'eighties and the 'nineties of the last century; that too many speeches, especially from the Front Bench, are hardly more than briefs read out by Ministers from a typescript prepared by their Departments; and that no experience has ever been quite so exciting as listening to a debate in which Mr. Gladstone participated when he was at the height of his form. On the first point, it is surely only necessary to say that the papers with mass-circulation did not exist when Sir Austen Chamberlain entered Parliament, and they have always made it a practice to pay little heed to the House of Commons save when its proceedings were news in the sense that a murder is news, or the result of a famous race, or a big boxing match, or the marriage of a member of the Royal family. As to the quality of debates, I think one must distinguish between one's memory of the great occasion, and the ordinary daily routine of regular public business. On the first, Sir Austen really meant that no one had ever impressed him so deeply as Mr. Gladstone at his best; that may well be true, even though he admitted later that he found it quite intolerable to read the very speeches of Mr. Gladstone he was so eager to praise. I can only say that, looking back on my own memories of debates, I would put, for general interest, the debates on the third reading of the Welsh Disestablishment Act of 1912, on the Savidge case in 1928, and on the position at Narvik in May 1940, as high, for their quality of argument and interest, as any debates I have ever read; and I draw from this the general inference that, as a rule, the great occasion is as likely as ever it was to produce the great discussion upon which the interest of the public will fasten.

I think it is even more true today than it was when Sir Austen Chamberlain testified in 1931 that far too many Ministers read their speeches from briefs prepared in the Departments; certainly, I have sat on many occasions in recent years in the gallery of the House listening to a Minister going through such pages, sometimes at a pace which made what he said almost impossible to follow, and sometimes with that kind of stodgy equality of emphasis which deprived what he had to say of any colour or character unless some sudden interruption threw him out of his stride, and led to a few minutes of exciting interchange of loaded words. In part, as Sir Austen Chamberlain himself said, when a brief may have important international repercussions, the Minister is entitled to stick close to his text; and, in part, the rules of the House

c

give the Speaker ample power to prevent the continuance of this evil habit, if he can be sure that he can count upon members generally to back him up. But I imagine that, even with all the power tradition has conferred upon him, the Speaker would not easily be persuaded to interfere with a Minister's statement unless he knew that to do so would not injure his reputation for impartiality, and that the House generally felt that the Minister was abusing his position. It is a very delicate duty to thrust upon the Speaker, and I doubt whether he would risk its performance save where his intervention involved someone upon the Front Bench who was unpopular with both sides of the House.

III

THE QUALITY OF THE HOUSE OF COMMONS

I do not share the view which regards with apprehension the decline and fall of the private member, and insists, with even greater apprehension, that Parliamentary control of the Executive, especially in the realm of finance, has become a nullity. Those who take this attitude are usually in opposition and, more usually still, playing the always agreeable role of *laudatores temporis acti*. I remember well, at a dinner at Lord Morley's house, about 1923, the host complained that the private member, in the post-1918 period, was reduced to a shadow of what he had been in the days of Mr. Gladstone, and how he was answered by Mr. Birrell, who reminded him of a dinner, at which they had both been present, with Mr. Gladstone in the later 'eighties when the great man, who had then been for nearly sixty years in the House of Commons, told his two younger colleagues that the private member of this generation was but a shadow of what the private member had been in what he evidently regarded as the golden age—the period between the Reform Act of 1832 and the disruption of the Conservative Party by Sir Robert Peel, when, in 1846, he shocked his party a second time by repealing the Corn Laws in complete disregard of its commitments. There is always a glamour connected with a past age—especially for the politician who is more liable than most other people to feel that he has been frustrated in the achievement of those high purposes which, had he but been given the chance, would have enabled him to change the course of history.

It is, of course, rare nowadays for the private member to initiate legislation which reaches the Statute Book, and he cannot even hope to do so unless the Government will find a place for his measure in its time-table. Everyone has heard of Sir Alan Herbert's success in changing the Divorce Laws and of Miss Ellen Wilkinson's achievement in ending some at least of the more outrageous practices in connection with the system of hire-purchase. But the number of members who have accomplished this feat is very small. The reasons are simple. First of all, the sheer volume of Government business in the modern state, as well as the range it covers, makes it highly unlikely that enough time will be found in the ordinary Parliamentary session for a repetition of the successes achieved by Sir Alan Herbert and Miss Ellen Wilkinson. I think that is wholly natural. Most matters that are important enough to be embodied in legislation should be the responsibility of Government for the simple reason that their very significance makes it virtually impossible to leave them in private hands. That it is desirable for some time in each session to be devoted to private members' motions, I should agree at once; but that, I think, is a way rather of securing public attention for a subject that the Government is neglecting than of enabling the member to promote a Bill because his subject secures support.

We are all asked to have pity for the private member because the crowded time-table of the House leaves him so little opportunity to speak, and so small a chance of influence in the division lobby when he does speak. I am all in favour of the fullest discussion possible of any measure in the House, or in one of its Committees. But it is not less imperative to bear in mind two things. First, the chances are great that when one of the major parties associates its fortunes with a big measure, the principles of that measure have long been a matter of vigorous debate, public and private, up and down the country. The raising of the school-leaving age, the nationalisation of the mines and the railways, had been, both of them, moving almost to the status of virtually agreed measures in principle for well-nigh a generation; and the final abolition of the Poor Law, which was finally achieved in 1948, under the aegis of the Minister of National Insurance, Mr. James Griffiths, had been put forward as desirable by Mrs. Sidney Webb and her co-signatories of the Minority Report of the Royal Commission on the Poor Laws as early as 1909. If you take a really big Bill, of first-rate importance, and give three full days to its second reading, I think you can

be assured that most of what can be said both for and
against its passage will have been said. Those whose views
we want to know by reason of their status in the leadership of their respective parties will pretty certainly have
told us the view they take, and, by a noble tradition of the
House, the Speaker is likely to protect the right of those
who hold irregular views about the matter to develop
their irregularities. As far back as 1930, it was being noted
that the then lone Communist member, the late Mr.
Saklatvala, had a special gift for catching the Speaker's
eye; and I think that the late James Maxton, in the last
House of Commons, and Mr. Gallacher in this one, could
hardly complain that they have been penalised because
they held their special views. Even within the fold of the
Labour Party, up to the period of his expulsion from it,
there must have been many members on the Government side of the House who envied not only the opportunities Mr. Speaker offered to Mr. Zilliacus, but even
more, the spacious way in which he took advantage of
them.

I see no sign of real deterioration in the character of the
House, least of all in the importance the House attaches
to those qualities—sincerity, courage and real knowledge
of the subject, the effort less to make an oration than to
debate incisively, a sense of humour—which go to make
up a member of the House at his best. I think it remains a
remarkable criterion of character, to be able to sift, with
great skill, the member who speaks deftly mainly in order
to make himself heard, from the member who may speak
badly, but is obviously trying to say something to which
he attaches real importance. It is rare for the House not

to be genuinely interesting at question-time, when what is really being investigated is the process of administration; and I doubt whether there is any other occasion in which the fitness of a Minister is so decisively tested, except, perhaps, when he is taking a Bill of which he is in charge through the Committee stage upstairs. But the House of Commons reaches its highest level when a government has got itself into a serious difficulty, through harshness or folly, or sheer lack of imagination, and is determined, regardless of some obvious error, to have its way in despite of the general condemnation it has earned.

There are three instances of this last situation to which I should like to refer. In 1923, Mr. (later Viscount) Bridgeman was Home Secretary, and in that capacity arrested, under the Restoration of Order in Ireland Act (1920), a large number of Irish extremists then resident in this country, and shipped them over to Ireland, where the Cosgrave Government put them into internment camps. One of the arrested men, a schoolteacher named Mr. Art O'Brien, sued on a writ of Habeas Corpus, on the ground that the Restoration of Order in Ireland Act (1920) had been inferentially repealed by the Irish Treaty Act of 1921. He won his case, so that the Home Secretary then became liable for damages to each of the arrested men for unlawful arrest and imprisonment, trespass, and a number of other matters. The Government of the day naturally introduced a Bill to indemnify Mr. Bridgeman against what was obviously a *bona fide* mistake on his part. Lord Robert Cecil (now Viscount Cecil) was put in charge of it. The Bill contained no provisions to compensate the arrested men for the unlawful detention to which they had been subjected; and though he was pressed to introduce such a clause when the Bill was in Committee from all sides of the House, Lord Robert not only refused to do so, but refused, if I may so phrase it, with some curtness of temper. The House began to get angry, and there developed that atmosphere of general attack on the Minister which the Whips always recognise as a red light of warning. Presently Mr. Baldwin, then the Prime Minister, came into the House, took his seat on the Treasury Bench, and listened carefully to a few speeches. Then, with that unerring flair for recognising a bad situation which was one of his greatest gifts, Mr. Baldwin rose and moved a short clause creating a judicial tribunal with powers to give compensation to any of the arrested men. Good-will was at once restored, and the remaining stages of the Bill had an easy passage. It was a moving demonstration by all parties of the view that when men have undergone unnecessary penalties at the hands of Government, even though the Minister concerned was sincere in the mistake he made, nevertheless it is the duty of the Government to compensate those who have suffered at its hands.

This was a relatively small occasion, though the principle involved was one of fundamental importance. My second case is not improbably one which did much to settle the future of this country in the second World War —I mean the famous Narvik debate of 1940. All of you will remember how a combination of follies and blunders led to our withdrawal from Norway, and its occupation by the Nazis. In the debate that followed this disaster, the Labour Party, then in opposition, decided to treat the adjournment motion on which the debate was taking place as a vote of censure. Its action won wide support from all sides of the House, and despite a plea by Mr. Neville Chamberlain, then Prime Minister, for support on personal grounds, and an eloquent though unsatisfactory defence of him by Mr. Churchill, then First Lord of the Admiralty, the errors of Mr. Chamberlain's policy were driven home so forcibly by Mr. Herbert Morrison, Mr. Lloyd George and Mr. L. S. Amery that a normal Government majority of over two hundred fell to eighty-one in a full House, many Conservatives abstaining from the division, and a number, some of whom had come back from the armies abroad for the occasion, voting against Mr. Chamberlain. His authority was broken by the debate; and though in the next two days he made an effort to restore it by widening the basis of his Coalition to include the Labour Party, the National Executive Committee of the Labour Party informed him that it would enter no Government of which he was the head, and that it regarded Mr. Churchill as the best available person to be Prime Minister. That is how Mr. Chamberlain felt himself bound to resign, and why Mr. Churchill was his successor. The curiously inept tale narrated by Mr. Churchill at the end of the first volume of his war memoirs in which he records the triumph of his leadership in the second World War has, I suppose, assumed its present shape only because of his unwillingness, after the General Election of 1945, to admit that the occasion of his glory in 1940 was made for him by the party which defeated him five years later. It may well be, as he suggests, that Mr. Chamberlain would have wished Lord

Halifax to become Prime Minister in his place, but none of the three men whom he describes discussing that wish in Downing Street could possibly, after the Baldwin–Curzon episode of 1923, have conceived that the wish would be fulfilled.

My third case is as recent as 1948. Most observers will, I think, agree that Mr. Ernest Bevin's policy in Palestine has not been the most shining aspect of his heavy labours. When, after the surrender of the British Mandate and the waging of that minor but still tragic war between the Israelis and the Arab states for the occurrence of which the responsibility of the Attlee Government is inevitably heavy, the Cabinet, obviously at the instance of the Foreign Secretary, sent British troops to Aqaba in what could not fail to look like a deliberate attempt to provoke, or at least to risk, an Anglo–Israeli incident there which might easily have led to fighting, Mr. Bevin lost most of what little credit he possessed with the House over his handling of the Palestine affair. In the debate which took place he cut a sorry figure, and was overwhelmed by the heavy fire of a dozen critics, notable among whom was Mr. Churchill. In spite of the strong support he received from Mr. Attlee—though it should be said that the con- viction the Prime Minister produced was in inverse pro- portion to the emphasis of his speech—the House had no real doubt that Mr. Bevin's policy was indefensible; and large-scale abstentions from its own side brought the immense Labour majority down to eighty. No one can really doubt that, as in the Narvik debate, this virtual defeat compelled a change in policy; for only a few days later the new state of Israel was given *de facto* recognition, and, shortly thereafter, formal diplomatic relations were established between the two countries. I should not like to say that this plain expression of feeling in the House of Commons has created in the Foreign Secretary a sentiment of effusive cordiality to Israel, but I do not think it is beyond the mark to suggest that Mr. Bevin has moved from passionate hostility to that typically British mood which begins to find good reasons for accepting as wholly natural a state of affairs which all his previous actions had sought to prevent from arising.

In all these aspects, I see no reason to suppose that the status of the House of Commons has deteriorated in the last fifty years. In none of them should I be prepared to admit the need of special remedies to meet a declining situation. It is the House which makes and unmakes Ministerial reputations. It is the House that watches with minute care the need for administration to be both just and reasonable. A Minister who persists in a policy against which the clear voice of the House has warned him will find, as a general rule, that his own party will criticise him as bitterly as the Opposition. The House knows almost by intuition those well-known types, the careerist, the man who talks merely for the sake of hearing his own voice, the man with a special hobby who brings it up as Mr. Dick brought up King Charles' head, and the crashing bore whose election to membership is a surprise, but whose re-election is something like a miracle. I think it is normally true that the House rises to the great occasion; and despite most complaints that every Opposition will make, it is usually true that from the passage of the second reading of a Bill to the stage where it is sent on to the

House of Lords, most things that need to be said both for and against it will in the course of debate be said. In general—Mr. Attlee is a notable exception—most members from the two front benches tend to speak too long, less, I suspect, because of what they have to say than because they think it disrespectful, both to the House and to their own positions, to occupy less than about forty minutes and upwards. It is, of course, true that there is a good deal of repetition in the run of speeches in any debate; but this is true of all debating assemblies, and could only be avoided by confining discussion to one speech on either side. I should agree that, in many subjects, the speeches of members, and even of Ministers, reveal that they are not expert about them; but members of the House of Commons are not elected because they are expert, and one of the most notable things in Parliamentary history is how rarely we find a really distinguished specialist successful in the kind of discussion for which the House of Commons is intended. After all, it is not a meeting of experts like, say, a gathering of members of the Chemical Society who have come to hear a paper on some aspect of chemical research, or of those members of the London Mathematical Society interested in the theory of numbers who have met in great excitement to hear someone of the calibre of the late Professor A. H. Hardy, or of the eminent Indian mathematician, Ramanujan, describe a new approach to the solution of Fermat's theorem. They are essentially a group of representative men and women, mostly not inherently notable in themselves, but clothed with a representative capacity by the constituencies which have sent them to the House of

Commons. With a small number of exceptions, they are not returned to Parliament for exceptional beauty of character, or distinction of mind; they have been returned there to support a party which their supporters hope will win enough seats to be able to form a government under the Premiership of its leader. The more fully we bear this in mind, the more clearly, I suggest, we shall understand what is the essential nature of the House of Commons.

IV

A REPLY TO MAJOR CRITICISMS OF PARLIAMENT

Anyone who reads even a small part of the recent literature on Parliament will find in it, in addition to the criticisms I have already dealt with, certain others upon which special emphasis is laid. The House of Commons, we are told, has lost its vital position as the watch-dog of the nation's expenditure; it can now hope only to sound its warnings when some indefensible wastage has already taken place. Since the publication, in 1929, of the late Lord Hewart's notorious pamphlet which he called *The New Despotism*, an increasing number of voices, specially from that powerful and well-organised trade union, the legal profession, tells us that the House of Commons has really lost the power of legislation to the Civil Service; all the bureaucracy permits it to do is to pass a framework of special principles which are made effective by the various Departments which make rules and regulations to bring them into life. Another line of attack is to insist upon devolution, sometimes territorial, as with the Welsh and Scottish Nationalists, sometimes functional, as in the proposals by Mr. and Mrs. Webb for a Political Parliament on the one hand, and a Social and Economic Parliament on the other; kindred proposals, less definite in form, have been made by Mr. Winston Churchill and, quite recently, by Mr. Christopher Hollis, the Conservative member for Devizes. The late Mr. F. W. Jowett, with the support of the then influential Independent Labour Party, urged for many years that the procedure of the House of Commons be remodelled so as to make it conform to that of a municipal council. He thought that this change would both speed up the passage of measures, and enable many more members to take an effective part in the work of the House. Many years after it had seemed that his proposals had been forgotten, they were revived by Sir Stafford Cripps, who has devoted a considerable essay to their defence. Nor must I omit to mention the persistent efforts of those who advocate the adoption of some form of proportional representation, or, though less ardently, of the alternative vote, on the ground that the present method both fails to produce a correspondence between the number of seats won by a party in the House of Commons and the number of votes they are given by the electorate, and that it operates against minor political groups with a specific point of view of their own. The present system is also said to be defective because it minimises the chances of men or women without party affiliation being returned to Parliament; and now that university seats have been abolished, it is argued that, regrettably, it will be still more rare for the member genuinely independent of the great party machines to find a constituency in which he can battle his way to victory against their influence.

I should like, briefly, to discuss all these criticisms, none of which, I would add, I find persuasive; and I then propose to put forward some criticisms of my own which I submit for your consideration. I cannot, in the first place, agree that the House of Commons should exercise a pre-natal control over Estimates; and I find it easy to understand why the Committee on Estimates, from which, a generation ago, some members hoped so much, has, in fact, been an obvious failure. In the first place, Estimates are the reflection of policy, and the making of policy is the function of the Cabinet, which seeks approval for what it proposes from the House. Once you give a committee or committees of the House any serious right to investigate Estimates, you take away from the Cabinet and from the Department the responsibility that is properly theirs. That can be seen by examining the parallel process in the United States Congress. There, in both Houses, a series of Committees examine, with what is often minute particularity, the proposals of each Department, not least in their financial aspects. They may make a cut here by the removal of some item they do not like; an obvious example is the lamentable decision which Congress took when, in 1943, it decided to abolish the National Resources Planning Board. Or they may insert an item by a process of give and take between members of a particular Committee which the Department itself feels to be quite unnecessary; it would be interesting to know how many federal buildings are due not to governmental needs but to the insistence of some powerful

member of the Committee that in the process of general
endowment his particular bailiwick should not be overlooked. Finance and policy cannot really be separated
from each other; and the Estimates Committee, even
with its sub-committees, can neither cover the range of
the Departments, nor hope to change seriously the mind
of a Minister who knows that he has the backing of a
Cabinet which, in its turn, knows that, in the last instance,
it can rely upon the loyal support of a majority in the
House of Commons. To make the Estimates Committee
a really successful instrument of control, it would need,
first of all, an official with a status like that of the Comptroller and Auditor-General, with a staff at his disposal
with the experience of the Treasury, which could count
on receiving Departmental Estimates sufficiently early to
be able to have examined them fully, and to have discussed them at length with the Minister and his officials in
time for these to reshape them in the light of such discussion before they were finally presented to the House of
Commons. Not only, as I believe, is this administratively
impossible, but it would eat into both the Minister's time
and responsibility in a way that would, in the long run,
alter the relations of legislature and executive quite fundamentally. I know nothing to suggest that this alteration
is possible; and, if it were, I know nothing to suggest that
it is desirable. And were it to be adopted in any thoroughgoing way, it would involve very grave and questionable
changes in the whole ethos of Parliamentary government.

A wise House of Commons, therefore, will, in my
view, be satisfied with the post-natal control it exercises
through the Public Accounts Committee, and that vital

officer of the House, the Comptroller and Auditor-
General. The fact that the latter is independent of the
Departments, that his scrutiny cuts deep and commands
wide respect, that he has, so to say, the visible authority
of the House behind him, gives him a mandate the power
of which makes his rulings, decisions, and suggestions
matters which the Treasury will see are fully honoured
by the different Departments. The reports of the Committee command great weight also; and there is massive
evidence to show that none of its conclusions go un-
attended, and that many of its proposals will be put into
operation after the Treasury has convinced itself that they
are workable. There is no external check upon Departmental habits which renders officials more scrupulous in
the economies that make wise spending. For, first of all,
they know that the Committee's investigation will have
been built upon a careful scrutiny of the evidence. They
know, in the second place, that full publicity will be
given to its findings, so that if they are denounced as
guilty of grievous error, they will get into trouble not
only with the House, but, in all likelihood, with their
own Minister, and the Treasury as well, that they will
have to find an answer to the Committee's charges, and
that they may well have to change traditional routines in
order to satisfy their critics. It is, no doubt, true that the
Committee is only able to cover a small area of the national
expenditure in each year; but there is obviously a healthy
respect for its operations even among the most eminent
civil servants whose long careers tempt them to regard
the outwardly majestic procession of their Ministers as in
fact hardly more than a march of transient and embar-

rassed marionettes, whom the eminent civil servants
themselves move in the proper direction. Anyone who
doubts all this, and is tempted to regard the House of
Commons, as an eminent Professor of this University regarded it, as a minor dependency of the Cabinet, a frustrated chorus of voices unable to choose its own songs,
even when it was permitted to sing at all, ought to read,
first of all, the remarkable Ninth Report of the Select
Committee on National Expenditure in the first World
War, and, secondly, the examination of Professor Muir
by the House of Commons Select Committee on Procedure in 1931. If I may say so, with all possible respect,
those who regard the House of Commons, in this connection, as a defeated regiment which has surrendered its
arms to its natural enemy, the Cabinet, have either never
been in the House of Commons at all, and are constructing a literary stereotype, like Bagehot's famous "retired
widow" at Windsor, or are politicians, sometimes politicians of great eminence who are, for some reason or
other, out of office when they think the country urgently
needs their services, and insist upon the powerlessness of
the House as a way of sublimating their own deep sense
of frustration. It is always urgent to remember, in reading
any account of the House of Commons by an eminent
Minister who is out of office when he wants to be back
there, that he is pretty certain to be glad to announce his
conviction that, while he is in opposition, the country is
bound to go to the dogs.

The growth of delegated legislation, with its consequential expansion of the sphere of administrative law,
has evoked, I am well aware, loud indignation from the

D

Bench and the Bar, and piteous cries from a number of members, most of them also in fact lawyers, that the rule of law no longer has any real meaning in Great Britain, and that the House of Commons has been compelled to transfer a large part of its authority to the Departments whose use of what is, in fact, the power to legislate is so exercised as to prevent the proper Parliamentary scrutiny of the use made of delegation. An irresponsible Lord Chief Justice, like Lord Hewart, and an academic lawyer whose hatred of change is even greater than his persuasive rhetoric, like Dr. C. K. Allen, are only the best-known names in a dramatic rear-guard action that has been fought for many years now against a phantom army of bureaucrats lusting for power which has never had any existence outside the imagination of those who warn us of impending doom and disaster. I can remember vividly that, when I was a member of the Committee on Ministers' Powers, I watched my colleague on that body, the eminent legal historian, Sir William Holdsworth, watching every witness from the Civil Service with anxious care to see if he could detect in the official mind a desire to amplify its jurisdiction beyond what was fit and proper. I do not think I am guilty of exaggeration if I say that the climate of Sir William Holdsworth's thinking did not lead him to regard radical innovation, whether against the historic supremacy of Parliament, or against the sacred right of the judges to interpret statutes, with anything that could fairly be called enthusiastic affection; I doubt, indeed, if I should go beyond the mark if I said that, for him, the Common Law had passed the zenith of its perfection, if not with Mansfield, then certainly with

Eldon. Yet at no point did it ever occur to Holdsworth to dissent from our *Report* which, whatever its weaknesses, did forthrightly conclude that delegated legislation is quite inescapable, and that there is no effective evidence to suggest that the Departments are seeking to abuse the rule-making powers which have thus been put into their hands.

Anyone who is sceptical of these conclusions might, before he rushes to hasty denunciation, peruse, and seek to answer, the two books, as learned as they are delightful, into which Sir Cecil Carr has distilled the quintessence of his incomparable experience. There is no need for me to traverse the ground which not only he has covered so admirably but which has been mapped, after the closest scrutiny, both of geological detail, and of natural and established fauna and flora, by my friends Professor W. A. Robson and Sir Ivor Jennings. On the side of this problem that concerns the delegation of rule-making powers, there are four simple facts that I wish merely to note. First, I would emphasise that the habit of delegation is not new; the House of Commons has not hesitated to use it any time in this last century and a quarter when it seemed clear that it was a convenient way of operating a statute efficiently. Second, the so-called "Henry VIII Clause" about which the critics have written as though it were the fount and origin of original sin, has not been employed a score of times altogether, and then quite unexceptionably either to bring a complex statute into efficient life, or to alter some minor detail which, on Departmental consideration, might have made it more difficult to give full effect at the proper time to the announced will of Parliament.

Third, it is remarkable to note that, except in emergency cases like an outbreak of foot-and-mouth disease, care is taken by the Departments to see that no Order or Rule is made until they have consulted every possible interest—and a good many impossible ones—affected by its promulgation. Fourthly, the House has not only the safeguard of the Select Committee which examines all proposed Orders and regulations; it has also the protection that the Act may require a confirmatory resolution to give effect to the use of the delegated power, or, save for emergency cases, it may require the proposed regulation to lie on the table of the House for periods that vary from 28 to 120 days. I know that many members of Parliament say, often with great warmth, that they cannot hope to prevail by means of a "prayer" against a regulation they dislike in a thin House, with the Whips on, and all of those present except the praying member himself anxious for nothing so much as the chance to go home as quickly as possible; but, I think the sufficient answer is that, after the brief debate on the prayer, it is the rarest possible occurrence for the very member who moves it to refer to the matter again. He has done what he was asked to do by those who brought the matter to his notice; and, having satisfied them of his energy and zeal in their service, he turns to other matters which he almost certainly regards as of outstandingly greater importance.

Nor am I convinced that the growth of an administrative jurisdiction in this country can be regarded as in any serious way an invasion of the rule of Law. Where Parliament, indeed, has deliberately conferred a policy-making power upon a Minister which involves him in the exercise of judicial functions, I should think it lamentable if the content of those powers were subject to judicial scrutiny with the result that technical points of procedure could be used to delay, even to prevent, the fulfilment of a purpose sanctioned by Parliament. On the evidence, above all since the famous *Arlidge* case, the judges seem to me to have used in their approach to most problems of administrative Law canons of statutory interpretation which have been intended not only to preserve the full amplitude of their jurisdiction over questions of *vires* but, also, to strike down in the realm of social policy changes in the direction the law has begun to take which they cannot easily reconcile with the doctrines that men like Holt read into the Common Law as they began to adapt it to the habits of a society increasingly dominated by the power of business men. It is a parallel tendency to that exhibited in their general attitude to trade union and industrial cases. Lord Esher said he could see no reason for the doctrine of common employment except the ingenuity of Lord Abinger in inventing analogies; I can see even less reason for judicial hostility like that of A. L. Smith, M.R., to the cases which arose out of the Workmen's Compensation Act of 1896—a hostility, you will remember, that required statutory rectification ten years later. Nor can one easily explain decisions like those in the *Taff Vale* case or in the *Osborne* case, or even in *Roberts v. Hopwood*, except upon the assumption that the judges have the right to build, as it were, a framework within the boundaries of which Parliament must confine its social legislation. There is a good deal to be said for the view that, in the past at least, the growth of administrative law is the outcome of a conscious judicial invasion of a sphere where novelty was intended by Parliament, and that the purpose of the invasion was to limit to the narrowest possible compass any novelty the judges might dislike.

Most observers agree that the working of administrative tribunals has been a great success. They are swift, they are expert in their work, and they are cheap. To allow them to fall under the control of the judiciary would have the effect of making the judges what they have become in the United States—effectively a third chamber of the legislature, with the power, as in the U.S. Supreme Court, to overrule legislative decisions at their discretion. I see no reason to suppose that this would help to safeguard the status of Parliament; on the contrary, as one saw in the first term of Mr. Roosevelt's Presidency, it is much more likely to lead to an unhappy conflict between the judges and Parliament, the first round in which would depend upon the source of judicial nomination, and the second upon an Act of Parliament which would reassert its sovereignty over any body which sought to rival its authority. I should like, indeed, to see a permanent court of appeal in administrative cases staffed by specialists in this quasi-judicial realm; they could give assurance that, in appropriate fields, such problems were dealt with in terms of a uniform procedure. But this apart, the less matters of political policy are transformed into judicial problems the less danger there is that judicial bias will enter into a realm where it has no place. If anyone is inclined to doubt this view, I suggest that the opinion of Lord Sumner in *Roberts v. Hopwood* will cure him of his scepticism.

There are then the proposals for devolution, whether national or functional. On behalf of the first, two major arguments are put forward. The first is the need to respond to the demands of Welsh and Scottish sentiment, and the second is the saving of time that would result if issues which concerned them alone did not occupy the time of the whole House. On the second argument I will say only that Mr. J. S. Henderson and I have elsewhere shown that the amount of Parliamentary time saved by national devolution is hardly even of the second order of importance; most of what is claimed for it could be quite adequately solved by leaving the application of United Kingdom Bills to Scotland and Wales to committees of the House of Commons composed of the relevant members who sit for each of these countries. Nothing that has been argued so far in favour of the creation of separate legislatures for each seems to me convincing. The economic unity of the three nations which make up the United Kingdom is so close that any serious movement in different directions would, I think, raise insoluble financial problems. A situation, for instance, in which there was a Tory Government in Westminster, and a Labour Government at Cardiff, might well mean the swift and unhappy movement of capital outside the borders of Wales. Different levels of taxation, different wage-rates, different factory legislation, would be utterly destructive of an organic economic unity which could only be destroyed at the price of serious economic loss. And when one remembers, first, that the necessities of the situation compel a unified foreign policy, which must be determined in Whitehall and in Westminster, and, second, that the major part of commercial relations cannot, on the international plane, be wisely separated from foreign policy, it seems to me beyond question that the kind of administrative devolution now symbolised by the Secretary of State for Scotland lies at the very margins of what we can attempt with either wisdom or safety. The decision, for example, whether or not to use Prestwick as a permanent alternative to London Airport, is, in essence, a technical, and not a national, question. If it can be shown that there is a good case, on economic and aeronautical grounds, for the permanent use of Prestwick as a viable alternative to London, it seems to me obvious that the recognition of Prestwick's value is beyond question. But I venture to suggest that the recognition of Prestwick, merely on the grounds of Scottish national prestige, and without regard to the problems of costs involved, would be a futile and expensive gesture which is not capable of defence on rational grounds. I agree, of course, that there are cases in which sentimental considerations justify putting economic arguments in the background. But I think the number of these cases is few; and I doubt whether they are sufficient in total importance to justify the creation of a special legislature for their effective regulation.

Functional devolution is, in our present phase of development, *prima facie* more attractive. Yet I am certain that all the proposals so far put forward involve insuperable difficulties. The proposal, for example, of Mr. and Mrs. Webb to divide legislative business into the political, on the one hand, and the social and economic, on the other, with a separate Parliament for each, leaves wholly unsolved the principle by which one category is effectively divided from another, the means by which the Parliament with the taxing power can be prevented from assuming an immediate supremacy over its rival, and the impossible difficulties in which we should become involved if there were a difference in the party complexion of the two Parliaments, with the result that the Government in each of them proceeded upon different postulates of action from the other. Mr. Churchill's proposal for an economic sub-Parliament leaves all these problems unsolved, and adds to them a number of new ones, not least the problem which, nearly three hundred years ago, Harrington tried to meet in his *Oceana* (1656) when he decided that one chamber should discuss legislation, and the other merely vote upon whether it was desirable or no; I find it hard to believe that any Assembly would accept a self-denying ordinance so wide that it resolved to accept or to reject statutes as the outcome merely of reading debates that have taken place elsewhere. There is, at any rate, no modern experience which could lead us to believe that we could embark upon such an adventure with any real hope of success.

The House of Industry, which has recently enchanted the agile mind of Mr. Christopher Hollis, is, as it were, an attractively designed vessel which is bound to sink as soon as it puts to sea. In his own account of it, Mr. Hollis does not, perhaps cannot, tell us what is the basis of industrial representation. Are the interests of Labour and Capital to be weighted equally? If not, what is the basis on

which their representation is to be settled? Is the occupation of the housewife—easily the largest single industry
in this country—to be represented in proportion to
numbers, or is it, as in the Economic Council of the
Weimar Republic, to be given a merely nominal representation which pays no heed to the reality of numbers? It
is relatively easy to see how the major industries can elect
their members to the "House of Industry" who, on the
special problems of those industries, can speak in the name
of their constituency. But it becomes far more difficult to
see how representation becomes really effective, in Mr.
Hollis' scheme, when a number of small, but quite distinct, industries have to be joined together in order to
make a viable constituency. It becomes even more difficult to grasp precisely how a candidate for election can
claim to represent his constituency unless he stands for
one of the normal parties to which we are accustomed. I
can see that a doctor who dislikes the National Health
Service can run against a doctor who strongly favours it;
but I am wholly unable to see any grounds upon which
a doctor, chosen by other doctors, could have a view, *qua*
doctor, of proposed developments in the mining industry. He might well have a medical view of the habits of
the Minister of Fuel and Power,[1] but that, surely, is a consideration built upon entirely different grounds from any
upon which he would be likely to seek election.

[1] In a speech at Hastings on the 26th of October, 1947, Mr. Gaitskell,
then Minister of Fuel and Power, discussed ways of saving fuel and said
"I've never had a great many baths myself, and I can assure those who
have as a habit that it does not make much difference to their health if
they have fewer." (Ed.)

I think, therefore, that Mr. Hollis' scheme would merely result in candidates offering themselves for election under the same auspices as now, but basing their appeal to constituencies organised as bodies of producers instead of upon grounds of simple geographical contiguity. That would, I think, raise two immensely complicated problems, to neither of which does Mr. Hollis offer any answer. The first is how he would safeguard the interests of consumers in a legislature of which the very essence is that it is concerned with the interests of producers. I emphasise the importance of this problem because I am unaware of any nationalised industry, whether it be coal, or transport, or the B.B.C., in which it has proved possible to find an institutional device for making the representation of consumers more than a nominal concept without any serious power of making their views carry real weight with the ultimate governing body which makes the vital decisions. The second is the difficulty—I should myself say the impossibility—of constructing a "House of Industry" without giving equal representation to employers and workers in each of the electoral units created. But if you once do this, you abandon the admirable Benthamite principle that, for voting purposes, each person shall count for one and not more than one, and you give special weight to the claims of property not to be adversely affected by the power of numbers. That is, of course, precisely what happened, under the Weimar Republic, to the German Economic Council. The result was that it was practically useless on all the large general issues, nationalisation, wage standards, hours of labour, and so on, but rendered quite useful service when a very specialised problem was referred to a small Committee of the Council, much as we refer such problems to a Select Committee of the House of Commons, or to a Royal Commission or a Departmental Committee. But that is not in the least what Mr. Hollis has in mind in urging upon us the importance of his "House of Industry". He is looking for the big decision, not the expert analysis which, over the whole field of Parliamentary business, is relatively a very minor affair. Though, therefore, I admire the enthusiasm and persuasiveness with which he argues his case, I am bound to conclude that his proposal cannot possibly secure the results to which he so eagerly looks forward. If I may so phrase it, his attempt to join the criticisms of Mr. Belloc to the inventiveness of Professor Cole results in a miscarriage as grievous as any I have noticed in modern times.

I need say but little of Mr. Jowett's proposals, to which, quite recently, Sir Stafford Cripps has given his approval. I think they fail because the committee system of local authorities from which they are derived has certain features quite different from anything in the House of Commons. It has limited terms of reference; its Council sits for a fixed term of years; and, in exceptional cases, chairmen of Committees in local authorities have influence, and a casting vote, rather than the immense powers which the political head of an important Department in the Central Government possesses. In an increasing degree, moreover, the policy of a local authority is made not so much in secret by an oligarchy composed of chairmen of Committees, the Council whips and the leader of the majority, as by the preliminary meeting of all the members in a private group whose decisions are taken to the Committees, and thence for confirmation by the Council as a whole. The chairmen of Committees, moreover, are chosen annually by the group, or groups, which have a majority; and they are directly assisted by the Council's officials at the meetings of their Committees. I find it very difficult to see how such a system could be applied to a body like the House of Commons, with no limited frame of reference. I cannot believe that it would be workable in the realm of finance, not less of appropriation than of supply, or in foreign affairs, or in defence matters. I do not see how a Chancellor of the Exchequer could reveal his budget proposals to perhaps a score of men and women, when he is not merely dealing with the need to lower or to raise a single tax, the rateable value of property, but is dealing with a multiplicity of taxes, prior information about which may well make fortunes for those who have it. I do not think that the essential work of a Foreign Secretary, not least his private correspondence with our diplomats abroad, could possibly be circulated to a committee of fifteen or twenty members many of whom are anxious to discuss the policies they reveal on the floor of the House of Commons. There is certainly also a period in the course of delicate negotiations where publicity could do a great deal of harm; and where the ability of a skilful journalist to extract an indiscretion from the member of such a committee as Mr. Jowett proposed might well have far-reaching effects. I do not say that diplomatic "indiscretions" have not on occasions done great good; but I am not convinced that we ought to provide an organised institution to assure their continuous appearance. What, moreover, is true of finance and foreign affairs is true also of defence. It applies also to a considerable area of work in the Home Office and the Ministry of Supply, to significant aspects of the Ministry of Labour, to Commonwealth Relations, and even to problems that have to be faced by the Ministry of Education. Closely examined, in fact, there are few of the major Ministries to which the committee system of local authorities could helpfully be applied.

On the other hand I think there is a good deal to be said for advisory Committees of the House of Commons to work with each Department. A good Minister would, I think, welcome the chance of a monthly meeting with such a body, to whose members he could explain what he was trying to do, or whose criticisms he could deal with forthrightly, without the limitations imposed upon them and him by the publicity of the House of Commons. As I conceive them, they would have no executive responsibility of any kind. But they would be useful to him by enabling him to test his policies upon a sample of public opinion before they have reached that stage where they can hardly be altered without a blow to his prestige, and they would serve the useful purposes of training members in the art of administration, of giving some real assurance that debate would be informed, and of bringing civil servants into direct contact with members of the Commons whom at present they do not always regard with too friendly an eye. I should like to see the Minister discuss regulations to be made under delegated powers with such a Committee before they were issued. In an informal way, also, I should like to see the Minister welcome suggestions from his Committee and have his appropriate officials discuss them with its members "without prejudice". There would, of course, have to be a limit to the number of such Committees upon which a member could sit, and an invariable right in the Minister to control its agenda. But I feel sure that there is here a field of immense possibilities to be explored; I am sure, for example, that such a Committee, sitting with Mr. Bevin on the Middle Eastern question, might well have helped to avoid some of the asperities of the discussions over Palestine. I am confident, also, that if a Committee of this type had the chance to put its views to the Prime Minister on the vital problems connected with atomic energy policy there would have been a good deal more flexibility than there has been in many of the statements made on our behalf at Lake Success. And if I may speak, for one moment, as one who has had nearly twenty-five years' experience of the Civil Service Arbitration Tribunal, I think that a good deal could be done by an advisory Committee of this kind in conjunction with the Treasury to work out, in the area of grading and of pay and conditions, principles which could help to improve relations which often seem lacking in imagination and common sense. At least I think it could have prevented the Chancellor from committing the obvious and egregious error of accepting the Masterman Report on the Political Activities of Civil Servants, before it had even been discussed at the National Whitley Council.

Since I am a strong believer in a stable executive with sufficient authority to drive an important and substantial

programme through the House of Commons in the lifetime of a Parliament of five years, I remain completely
unconvinced by the advocates of Proportional Representation, in any of its numerous forms, or of kindred
expedients like the alternative vote. I do not think it is
important that, from time to time, a minority of the electoral votes may give a party a majority of seats so that
it is able to form a government. For it would be a very
stupid party, obviously courting defeat, which failed to
remember that it must not outrage the Opposition, that
it must show a real respect for a minority of importance,
and that it must pay careful attention to the currents and
cross-currents of opinion outside the House of Commons. P.R. has a centrifugal effect which encourages
looseness of discipline, excessive compromise, the politics,
if I may so phrase it, of manœuvre rather than of policy,
and a continuous threat to the stability of executive
power. I think it largely, though by no means universally,
destroys the intimacy of relation between the member of
a legislative assembly and his constituents. So far as I
know, it invariably increases the power of the party
machine, and thus reduces the independence of the member. On its premisses, no doubt, P.R. is far more logical
than the system by which we choose members of Parliament. But as I do not accept those premisses I find the
logic far less impressive than do the advocates of the
system.

The premisses, I think, are two in number. They are,
first, that Parliament should be a mirror of national
opinion, and, second, that its members should represent
that opinion in proportion to the number of electors who

support any given outlook. A number of supporting inferences indeed are brought forward to strengthen these: the danger of majority tyranny, the excessive authority of the party whips, the value of the independent member who can give undivided allegiance to his own conscience. None of these, however, is so important as the two major premisses to which I have referred, and I should like to say a word about each of them. Even with universal suffrage, I do not believe that there is any real substance in the view that Parliament should be a mirror of national opinion. For, first of all, there are many matters, and these matters of real importance, upon which no national opinion exists; and, second, there are many matters which are vital to the life of our people a judgment upon which is impossible in an electorate of some thirty million people. That is not all. There are moments when the electorate is in a frenzy of divided excitement about some issue that is quite transient in character—the Tichborne case, for example, or the Zinoviev letter, which played so large a part in the General Election of 1924—and there are matters about which the people may feel keenly without it being wise for any public action to be taken in Parliament, of which a good example is, I think, the internal life of churches, which is, as a general rule, best left to the appropriate governing bodies of the churches themselves to determine. Lord John Russell illustrated this admirably when, in response to the clamour over the restoration of the Roman Catholic hierarchy in this country in 1851, he passed the Ecclesiastical Titles Act to prevent Roman Catholic prelates from assuming, like the Archbishop of Westminster, for example, territorial titles without the

E

authority of the Crown; with wide popular approval, moreover—for ardent Protestants still felt the heat from the fires of Smithfield—he put into the Act heavy penalties against any proud prelate who should offend against its provisions. Nevertheless, Cardinal Wiseman still continued to call himself Archbishop of Westminster, and no one ever thought of giving effect to the statute. Not a whisper was heard from anyone when Mr. Gladstone quietly repealed the Act in 1871.

The first and most vital function of the electorate is to choose a House of Commons the membership of which makes possible the creation of a Government which can govern. Its second function is to criticise or support the policies of the Government it has created, and, where it thinks fit, to compel some member of the Government, or the whole Government, if necessary, to resign, or, it may be, to appeal from a hostile vote in the House of Commons to the voters in a new general election in which it seeks, if it can, to gain a renewal of its authority. It is because these are its major functions that the electorate needs to be divided in such a way that the House of Commons that results from its choice can perform them effectively. It is the great merit of our system that, as a general rule, it has usually, at any rate since 1832, been successful in attaining those purposes. No doubt the party system, as we know it, has a special pathology of its own. It is hostile to the independent member; it makes the rise of new parties a difficult matter; it secures a general vote of confidence in men rather than a mandate upon measures; and, once it has brought the new House of Commons into being, the character of its party pattern gives both the House and the electorate a Government which party discipline will usually maintain in office for a period pretty close to the five years set as its legal term by the Parliament Act of 1911. There may, indeed, be special cases, as in 1924 and 1929, when the Government does not command a majority in the House; and grave crises, as in the two world wars of 1914 and 1939, or the flight from the pound in 1931, may create circumstances in which parties combine to form a Coalition Government on the ground that some overwhelming need transcends the normal differences which keep one party in office and one in opposition. On experience, however, I think most observers would agree that minority government is almost always bad government. There is no effort at long-term thinking; the Ministers are mainly preoccupied in manoeuvres which will enable the Prime Minister to secure a dissolution from the Crown upon an issue his party's attitude to which will find favour with the electorate. Minority government is invariably uneasy government, and usually it is cowardly government. Few Cabinets built from a minority party will put before the House a clear and coherent body of measures; their real anxiety is to make sure that their defeat comes upon a measure the popularity of which seems to them beyond doubt. They are therefore always weak Governments since they are always evading the measures they believe to be necessary whenever they suspect these are likely to prove unpalatable. And they breed much the same temper in their opponents. The main object of the latter is to catch a minority Government in a trap, preferably of its own making. That is what happened to the minority

Labour Governments both in 1924 and 1931; and, in each case, this created an evil psychological atmosphere which did harm not only to the morale of the party leaders, but to that of the electorate as well. The deterioration of Ramsay MacDonald's character after he first became Prime Minister is notorious; and I do not think I am mistaken in discovering in the electors who gave Mr. Baldwin a majority, after the defeat of the Labour Government of 1924, an indecision, a readiness to be stampeded by irrelevancies, for which it later paid a heavy price.

"England", said Disraeli, "does not love coalitions"; and, in a general way, that typical utterance of his shows his usual insight into the character of our people. But I think we must make a distinction between Coalition Governments in war-time, when they emphasise the national determination to unify its striking-power, and Coalition Governments in peace-time, which usually represent the effort of politicians to compromise principles in the hope of retaining power. Certainly, in my own view, both the Asquith Coalition of 1915 and the Lloyd George Coalition of 1916 were essential stages in evolving the necessary instrument of victory in 1918; I do not think the Liberal Government which entered the first World War of 1914 would have been able to preserve authority enough over four years to impose the measures which the situation demanded. I hardly think that Mr. Chamberlain's Government from 1939 to 1940 can properly be called a Coalition; for it is obvious that, although he secured the accession to his Cabinet of Mr. Churchill and his friends, the Labour Party, then the official Opposition, refused to join him because it had no confidence in his leadership. But few people here can have forgotten, or will ever forget, how, when the Labour Party agreed to serve under Mr. Churchill, as Prime Minister, in May of 1940, there came an inspiring change in the spirit of the whole nation, which, after some weeks, communicated itself to that not inconsiderable section of the Tory Party which, as Mr. Churchill himself has told us, sat sullen and resentful in the House of Commons when the new Prime Minister explained the policies of his Cabinet, and reserved their cheers for Mr. Neville Chamberlain whose disastrous foreign policy had compelled the Labour Party to remain aloof from any Government of which he was the head.

The situation of a Coalition Government in peace-time raises very different issues. Let us examine the two outstanding experiments of this kind, and the effort towards making a third, to which Mr. Winston Churchill devoted his immense persuasive powers in those months of the spring of 1945 when the Germany of Hitler was being broken in pieces by the combined effort of the Allies. The Armistice of the first World War was signed on 11th November 1918, and it was followed in a few weeks by the dubious "coupon election", in which Mr. Lloyd George, with the small handful of Liberals, two or three Labour men, and the half-dozen self-styled "detached" persons who belonged to no political party, like for instance, the late Sir Eric Geddes, joined with the full Conservative Party, to fight as a united organisation against the Labour Party, which had just been given its "new look" by the joint skill of Mr. Arthur Henderson and Mr. Sidney Webb, and the independent Liberals who refused to follow Mr. Lloyd George's lead, and gave their allegiance to Mr. Asquith. To the candidates who gave assurances that they would support the war-time Coalition Government of Mr. Lloyd George, a special letter of recommendation was given; and the electorate was urged to vote for these candidates on the ground that the Coalition which had won so overwhelming a victory had both the skill and the experience so necessary for the work of reconstruction and peace. The appeal was overwhelmingly successful; the supporters of the Coalition won 472 seats in the House of Commons, compared to the 130 won by their opponents, though it should be added that they gained only fifty-two per cent of the votes cast as against the forty-eight per cent polled by the two parties in the Opposition.

Two things, moreover, showed very quickly that the Coalition victory had been snatched from the ill-considered emotion of relief at the victory over Germany. First of all, the Government began, almost at once, to lose by-elections. Secondly, it began to speak with several voices at the same time, often at variance with one another. Mr. Winston Churchill, for instance, announced that the railways were about to be nationalised, a view which was promptly repudiated by his leaders. Then, to avert a national strike by the mineworkers, Mr. Bonar Law announced the appointment of the Sankey Commission the report of which he agreed, in the House of Commons, to accept "in the letter and the spirit"; but when the Commission reported in favour of the nationalisation of the mines, the Government promptly repudiated his pledge. In the peace conference at Versailles, the need for a sensible treatment of Germany over the issue of reparations, which Mr. Lloyd George learned to understand pretty quickly, was overwhelmed by a demand from more than 350 of the Government's supporters in the House of Commons that Germany should pay the major costs of the war; the result was to set Germany on the path that led inexorably to the victory of Hitler. Then came the sudden fear of inflation in 1921; and the notorious Geddes Committee was appointed to economise on national expenditure, with the result that the Coalition lost immensely in popularity, especially with the workers, by destroying most of the progressive social legislation, like Mr. Fisher's Education Act, upon which so many hopes had been founded. There then developed deep disagreement in the Cabinet over policy towards Russia and the Middle East, especially when, in 1922, Mr. Lloyd George's enthusiasm for the Greece of Venizelos brought us very close to the danger of war with Turkey. At that point, the majority of the Tories could accept Mr. Lloyd George's leadership no longer; and at an historic meeting at the Carlton Club, Mr. Bonar Law, supported by Mr. Baldwin, though strongly opposed by Lord Birkenhead and Mr. (later Sir) Austen Chamberlain, carried a motion in favour of ending the Coalition Government. From 1922 until 1931, this country returned to party government in the strict sense of the term.

The history of the "National" Government of 1931 has not yet been fully told; but we know enough of it to recognise the light it throws on coalition government in peace-time. The crisis which created it grew out of a flight from the pound which it is now pretty generally agreed was not the fault of the Labour Government, but of that world depression of which the impact on the United States in October 1929 was perhaps the most striking illustration. To stop the drain on our gold reserves, a loan was sought from the Federal Reserve Board in Washington, and this was agreed to by the Board on condition that the British budget was balanced. This involved cuts in expenditure; but when it was proposed to reduce unemployment pay by ten per cent, Cabinet disagreement was so profound that the Government, which was in a minority in the House of Commons, decided that resignation was its only possible course. In agreement with his colleagues, the Prime Minister, then Mr. Ramsay MacDonald, went to Buckingham Palace to resign, and with the intention of recommending that he should be replaced by the leader of the Opposition, Mr. Baldwin. He later informed his astonished colleagues that he had become the Prime Minister of a Coalition Government in which Mr. Baldwin, the Conservative leader, and Sir Herbert Samuel, the acting leader of the Liberal Party, would serve under him; and he found places in his new Ministry for Mr. Philip (later Viscount) Snowden, for Mr. J. H. Thomas, and for Viscount Sankey, while some sixteen members of the Labour Party in the House of Commons transferred their allegiance to him, in his new role. Mr. MacDonald explained to a meeting of the Under-Secretaries in his Labour Government that the change he had made was a temporary expedient merely, intended to last for about six weeks, and undertaken to prevent Great Britain from going off the gold standard.

We have, as yet, no official knowledge of what transactions took place at the Palace which resulted in this extraordinary change. I myself believe that the effective source of the change was the influence of King George V, though I think Mr. MacDonald himself, as well as Mr. Baldwin, had contemplated the possibility of such a development as early as November 1930. It is only fair, I think, to note that, in a published account, Mr. Sidney Webb does not share my view that the King directly interfered to bring about the remarkable arrangement, and that a careful authority, Sir Ivor Jennings, supports Mr. Webb. Whatever the origins of this Coalition its subsequent history is not in doubt. Formed to keep Great Britain on the gold standard, it broke loose from gold a month later. It then dissolved Parliament, and went to the country asking for what it termed a "doctor's mandate", arguing, no doubt in deference to Mr. Snowden and its Liberal members, that it would not erect a protective tariff in Great Britain without a full and impartial enquiry, and that its defeat would be fatal to all savings, even to those of humble people with a few pounds in the Post Office. In a fantastic broadcast, Mr. Snowden described the financial proposals in the Labour Party's election programme as "Bolshevism run mad", while a considerable number of Tory candidates insisted in their election addresses, and on the platform, that every vote cast against them was a vote against the King. Mr. Ramsay MacDonald himself, who had become, as he explained to Mr. Snowden, the favourite of all the duchesses in London, toured the country waving worthless German million-mark notes, and declaring that, if he were defeated, the pound would become as worthless as the mark had been during the incredible period of German inflation, in 1923, when most German savings, especially of the small bourgeoisie, were wiped out. By a combination of confusion and fear, the electorate was stampeded into an overwhelming victory for Mr. MacDonald, who, in fact, was serving merely as a front for Toryism; the Labour Party, which had held 289 seats in the Parliament of 1929, was reduced to 56, and, save for Mr. George Lansbury, Mr. Attlee and Sir Stafford Cripps, all its best-known leaders were defeated. Almost at once, and without even the pretence of the "impartial" inquiry that had been promised, a protective tariff was introduced, Mr. Snowden (who had gone to the House of Lords) and the Liberal members of the Government being allowed to ease their consciences by the famous "agreement to disagree" which permitted them both to speak and vote against the tariff despite its introduction by a Cabinet to which they belonged. When, a year later, Mr. Baldwin secured the acceptance of Imperial Preference at the Ottawa Conference, the Liberal Ministers finally split. Some of them, like Sir Herbert (now Viscount) Samuel and the late Sir Donald Maclean, resigned, as did Viscount Snowden, who had always been a passionate advocate of free trade; others, like Sir John (now Viscount) Simon, who had formed themselves into Liberals with the suffix "National" to indicate their support of the National Government, adjusted themselves with surprising speed to the new outlook; though they remain, formally, a separate organisation, they are now, to all intents and purposes, a minor dependency of the Tory Party. After Snowden and his Liberal colleagues left the Cabinet, it became, for all its claim to national status, essentially the normal Tory Government, presided over, with diminished authority, by Mr. MacDonald until he made way, in 1935, for the last period, in which Mr. Baldwin held office.

There are two important characteristics in this Coalition that are worthy of notice, the one in the domestic, the other in the international, field. In the first, the Government passed a good deal of legislation which, in perspective, looks very like an effort to evade the need for discussion in the House of Commons. The Tariff Commission, for example, could itself propose higher rates of duty, and Parliament agreed that the Ottawa preferences could not be altered without the consent of the Dominions, even though the Dominions accepted no parallel responsibility for imports from Great Britain. The fate of nearly three million unemployed was put into the hands of the Unemployment Assistance Board, which, in all its major features, was made independent of Parliamentary control. A number of Marketing Boards were established with rights of their own so far-reaching that there was given to some of them a criminal jurisdiction not unlike that of the Star Chamber. The mutiny in the Navy at Invergordon led the Government to pass an Incitement to Disaffection Act which, though drastically altered by criticism both in the House and out of it, still resembled, when it had reached the Statute Book, the kind of legislation normally to be expected from foolish and terrified Ministers like Lord Sidmouth. And to this must be added a view of the Official Secrets Act so far-reaching that, under its clauses, Mr. Duncan Sandys could be threatened with its penalties by the Secretary for War and the Attorney-General for asking a question in the House which revealed the unsatisfactory state of the Government's preparation against the possibility of hostile attack from a foreign power.

This semi-totalitarian attitude—of which it is well that we should remind ourselves—was closely related to the remarkable change in foreign policy which the "National" Government effected between the large-scale Japanese aggression against China in 1931-2 and the final destruction of the rump of Czechoslovakia on 15 March 1939. In those years, in flat opposition to public opinion, the "National" Government, under three successive Prime Ministers, not only refused to honour its obligations under the Covenant of the League of Nations, but steadily moved to a position where it was but a hair's breadth removed from an effective alliance with all the reactionary powers in Europe as well as with Japan. It would do nothing for China over Manchukuo. It was a large factor in the failure of the Disarmament Conference. Despite its pledges at the General Election of 1935, it did not pursue an effective policy of sanctions against Italy during Mussolini's attack on Abyssinia, and, indeed, finally acquiesced in recognising his annexation of it. When General Franco rebelled against the constitutional Republican Government of Spain, it took the lead in the futile policy of non-intervention, and thus not only helped to establish Fascism in Spain, but lied every week to the House of Commons by denying any knowledge of what everyone else knew, that Hitler and Mussolini had troops, aeroplanes, tanks, heavy guns and munitions there,

and continued to supply Franco despite the fact that they
were both pledged to non-intervention. They refused any
support to France when Hitler remilitarised the Rhine-
land. They allowed Hitler to seize Austria without more
than verbal protest. Then came the crowning infamy of
Munich and its sequel, a betrayal so gigantic that it was
visible to the self-blinded eyes of the Prime Minister, Mr.
Neville Chamberlain. When he awoke to the fact that his
policy had endangered democratic institutions throughout Europe by his acquiescence in the expanding power
of Hitler and Mussolini, who had by then seized Albania,
he gave guarantees of territorial integrity to the semi-
Fascist states of Poland, Greece and Rumania. Since there
was no easy and direct way in which the "National"
Government could implement the guarantees he had
given, especially that to Poland, it sought to achieve, in a
curiously leisurely way, a treaty of mutual assistance with
the Soviet Union, though even then, it was still trying,
at the same time, to come to a large-scale commercial
agreement with Hitlerite Germany. By the time that the
British Mission, which contained not merely no Minister
of the Crown but not even an official of the first rank,
had begun its discussions, the Russians had already made
up their minds that Chamberlain was not too eager for
their successful outcome, since he was not even willing to
persuade Poland to permit Russian troops to cross Polish
territory to halt a clearly impending German attack. The
Russians, therefore, with grim realism, broke off their
negotiations with the British Mission, and proceeded to
conclude the fatal non-aggression pact with Hitler which,
by freeing him from the fear of an attack on Germany

both from the East and the West, rang up the curtain on the second World War.

From whatever angle the Coalition of 1931 is regarded it is difficult not to argue that it was a dangerous threat to Parliamentary institutions. If it is said that the Labour Opposition was not good enough to make a real impact upon public opinion in debate, that it could not, even over a matter as dramatic as the murder of Jarrow by an affiliate of the Bank of England, it still remains true that the international policy of Mr. Chamberlain caused the resignation of Mr. Anthony Eden and Lord Salisbury (then Viscount Cranborne) at one stage, and Sir Alfred Duff Cooper at another; and, whatever the mistakes in Mr. Churchill's judgment of the Spanish and the Italian issues, however clear his hatred of Russia and its communism, he spoke against the threat to Great Britain of Hitler's monstrous tyranny in a mood which, for fervour and passion, was like nothing so much as the furious attack of Burke against the implications of the French revolutionary wars. Yet it is obvious that his attack made no impression on the "National" Government until after the final destruction of Czechoslovakia in March 1939, and relatively little impression on public opinion outside Parliament until, a few days after the betrayal of Munich, the sense of its brutality and shame took an unbreakable hold of the British people.

The danger of the "National" Government formed in 1931 was built upon a number of factors. The first was that it bred a confusion in the public mind, based upon intrigues the secret of which it had no means of penetrating, which destroyed its power of judgment. Many years

of eager propaganda had built up MacDonald and Snowden as the two major symbols of socialism; the election of
1931 was long over before any important part of the
unattached voters began to realise they had betrayed
principles they had professed to serve for most of their
lives. The confusion, of course, was deepened, when
MacDonald not only secured Liberal support for his effort,
but was able to retain the aid of leading Liberals long after
the official Liberal Party had realised that its members,
also, were the victims of a skilfully executed conspiracy.
The second factor was the deep sense of dismay amongst
the electorate, not only at the failure of the second Labour
Government to tackle with any courage the grave
economic problems which confronted it, but also at the
grim spectacle of the distressed areas with what seemed
like their permanent mass of unemployed for whom there
seemed no prospect of work in the future. Dispirited men
and women, with children who are often hungry, and
often so shabbily clothed that their parents are ashamed to
send them to school, soon begin to lose hope; and, since
hope is one of the pillars of Parliamentary democracy, as
it shrinks, it makes for an inertia unfavourable, both in the
House of Commons and out of it, to the kind of challenge
that makes a Government respect the force of public
opinion. Nor must it be forgotten that the "National"
Government expressed the drift of a large part of Europe
from a faith in democratic institutions towards a half-
suspicion that, perhaps, there might be something in the
pattern of the *Führer-prinzip* the secret of which Parliamentary government had lost. A further factor, as I
believe, was the failure of the Labour Party, in its years

of opposition from 1931 to 1939, to drive home clearly
the implications of the "National" Government. It probably spent almost as much energy, once the General
Election of 1931 was over, in fighting the Communists as
in fighting the Tories; and it seemed to have lost the drive
and the convictions that shone so brightly in the propaganda of Keir Hardie and Blatchford before 1914, and
of George Lansbury after it. There was a curious timidity
about its effort to arouse the workers in years when all the
conditions seemed set for the rise of a new Chartist
Movement; and it seemed resentful of any other effort to
do so that was not commenced under its own auspices.
It is, in fact, difficult not to believe that the Labour Party
itself was so unnerved by the events of 1931 that it did not
recover from their effect until the grim martyrdom of the
Spanish Republic began the renovation of its own spirit
and vision.

The Labour Party, in those years of the "National"
Government, was unsuccessful in the House of Commons
because on domestic matters it did not look beyond the
division lobby where it accepted frustration as its inevitable fate. It never attempted to organise any effective
pressure on the Government outside the House of Commons; nothing here is more typical than its attitude of
sullen resentment against the dramatic march from Jarrow
of the unemployed in which Miss Ellen Wilkinson played
so brave a part. But in relation to foreign affairs it was
hardly more imaginative. It was devoted, more strongly
than any other party, to the method of collective security
against any aggressor based upon a loyalty to the Covenant of the League of Nations which overrode any con-

siderations of domestic expediency. But, historically, it was also a party with a strong vein of pacifism in its composition, a deepening of hostility to conscription, and an ardent desire to further the cause of disarmament. It was, therefore, in a perpetual dilemma over foreign policy. It sought to lead the League in hostility against the use of war as an instrument of national policy; but it was compelled to accept the view of many members that sanctions must not be employed by the League lest they should lead to war. It could not support conscription, and it therefore informed both its friends and its enemies that if, as in 1914, it were driven to fight, it would be at least two years before it could play its full part against the aggressor. It was strongly opposed to the foreign policy of the "National" Government, and it therefore voted, year by year until 1937, against the defence estimates. Each of these attitudes caused a good deal of bewilderment. The alternative to conscription was, as everyone knew, a professional long-service army recruited by starvation. Though socialists knew that the vote against the defence estimates was, in fact, a token vote against the policies of the "National" Government, it was always represented as a refusal to give the country armament proportionate to its strength and purposes; and there was a very large number of voters in the inter-war years who, when they read the pacifist speeches of Labour members in the House of Commons, or read, in the light of Nazi and Fascist expansion, of their attacks against the Admiralty or the War Office or the Air Ministry for making impossible demands upon the Exchequer, felt that a party so divided on defence policy could not be safely entrusted

F

with power; and this inner contradiction in the party's outlook persisted until within a few weeks before the outbreak of the second World War.

To the climate of mental confusion thus engendered under the "National" Government must be added the emphasis given to it by the attitude of the Trades Union Congress General Council, then, as now, in close affiliation to the Labour Party. After the brief experience of militancy during the general strike of 1926, the Council embarked, first, on a futile consideration of collaboration between workers and employers, the so-called Mond–Turner period, and then upon a return to the unimaginative routine of the pre-1926 epoch, in which its chief purpose seemed to be the repression of any militant policy among the unemployed lest this be taken as an index of sympathy for Communist ideas. The result was that, after the bitterly fought election of 1931, the trade union leaders hardly gave any leadership to their members, least of all to those who, like the unemployed, needed it most. The inevitable result was a considerable infiltration of Communist ideas into many of the largest unions; in the miners, the transport workers, the railwaymen and the engineers important executive positions were won by the Communists. But the exclusion of the Communists from any of the political relations of the trade unions meant either that they sought to build their own political groups in the unions, which acted as a divisive influence, or that they used their position to undermine the consideration in which the Labour Party, and even more, the Parliamentary form of democracy, was held. The combination of Tory self-confidence, due in part to its overwhelming

ascendancy in both Houses of Parliament, and the realisation among the masses, that, in the face of such an
ascendancy, relatively little could be done to ease their
position, certainly led, between 1931 and Munich, to a
curious decline of belief in the value of Parliamentary
institutions. That is shown by the sharp decline of votes
cast in the elections of those eight years. It was only when
Munich revealed the depth of the crisis Great Britain
confronted that the recovery of interest began to display
itself in unmistakable terms.

I suggest, therefore, that the peace-time Coalition of
1931 did serious harm to the status of Parliament. It is in
the light of this harm that we must consider Mr.
Churchill's attempt to continue, after the victory in
Europe, the war-time Coalition Government he had so
remarkably led from May 1940 until May 1945. In the
whole of that period there had been an electoral truce,
by which the parties to the Coalition had bound themselves not to contest seats against one another; there had
therefore been no general election for ten years, and in the
by-elections which occurred during the five years of
Mr. Churchill's Premiership only an occasional election
had been fought by Communist candidates, or a member
of the independent socialist group which called itself the
Commonwealth Party, or an independent candidate with
some special programme of his own. By the Parliament
Act of 1911, of course, there ought to have been a general
election not later than the Spring of 1940, but, with
general assent, power had been taken by Parliament
to prolong its own life year by year during the war.
When Mr. Churchill himself moved for a further year's

prolongation in the late autumn of 1944, he recognised
that this was an unsatisfactory position, and, in emphasising
his view that there ought to be a general election as soon
as possible after victory in Europe, he expressed the hope
that this would be the last year in which he would have
to ask for any further prolongation. But, in the early
Spring preceding the final German surrender, he proposed both to the Labour and Liberal leaders in his
Government that the Coalition should be continued,
either until the victory over Japan was complete, or for
eighteen months, whichever was the shorter period. It is
not entirely clear whether Mr. Churchill envisaged a
new "coupon" election, like that of Mr. Lloyd George
in 1918, or whether he was proposing simply the continuance of his Government in power for a maximum period of eighteen months, subject to the approval
of this procedure by the electorate at the special refer-
endum on the matter which he suggested might be
taken to strengthen the authority of the Government
should the Labour and Liberal Parties approve his proposal.

In any case, the Labour Party's National Executive
Committee rejected Mr. Churchill's offer by a decisive
vote, immediately and overwhelmingly endorsed by the
National Conference of the Party; though there was a
suggestion that the Coalition should continue until
October, when the life of the Parliament elected in 1935
would end without a new Act for its renewal. This would
have enabled the Coalition to separate into its component
parties with a dignity worthy of the great triumph it had
achieved; it would also, though this was then, of course,

unknown, have enabled Mr. Churchill to remain Prime Minister until the end of the war against Japan.

Mr. Churchill curtly refused this offer. He broke up the Coalition at once, replacing its Labour and Liberal members by members of his own party, and announced a dissolution of Parliament at once. The result of the General Election was an overwhelming Labour victory, the party obtaining 394 seats, and succeeding, up to the end of November 1949, in holding them without the loss of a single by-election in over four and a half years of office —a record in the modern history of Parliament. The political battle thus resumed its party character, and it is not unfair to say that it aroused an interest, both intellectual and emotional, as great as in any period since 1832. I think it is also just to say of the election campaign itself in 1945, despite Mr. Churchill's own effort to make it a "stunt" campaign, on the model of the "Red Letter" election of 1924, or the "threat to your savings" election of 1931, that few people can remember an election at which the level of discussion was higher, or in which the voters seemed more aware of the important decisions they were taking. The average poll was very high; the election meetings were usually packed to overflowing; and, despite the immense personal hold Mr. Churchill's war leadership naturally and rightly won for him in all classes of the population, the most interesting features of the election were, first, the swiftness with which it became a judgment on Tory policy in the pre-war years, and, second, the size of the support for the Labour Party among the armed forces at home and abroad. It was a decision made by a people which had made up its mind what it wanted to do. On all the evidence, moreover, it appears highly probable that this mood of seriousness has persisted throughout the years since 1945.

War apart, therefore, a Coalition Government seems to me to inflict injury upon the process of Parliamentary government. It blurs responsibility, it prevents the issues being clearly defined, and it hampers their realistic discussion. Mr. Ramsay MacDonald's conception of the ideal Parliament as a Council of State—in which the Opposition co-operates with the Government for the common good—seems to me to come near to opening the door to the one-party state; and the nearer we approach, even by consent, to that condition, the more likely we are to destroy the essential virtues of Parliamentary democracy, which rests, above all, upon the full freedom of constitutional opposition. Nor can I accept the view, so strongly advocated by Professor Ramsay Muir, that minority government is desirable because it compels the party in office to win the support of members of parties in opposition. Professor Muir seems to think that, by this means, we shall get a nationally acceptable policy from Parliament; and he points to the record of the Social Democratic Government in Sweden as the proof of his argument. I do not think he is right on either count. Granted our own Parliamentary tradition, a series of minority Governments would rapidly lead either to some form of coalition government, the peace-time undesirability of which I have already discussed; or it would lead to a situation in which the minority Government's defeat would lead its Prime Minister to ask for, and probably be granted, the right to a dissolution in the hope that a general election would give him and his party a majority in the new House. When, after the General Election of 1923, Mr. Asquith and the Liberals supported the Labour vote of "no confidence" in Mr. Baldwin, which led to the accession to office of the first Labour Government, he did so upon two assumptions. The first was that he and his party could prevent the Labour Government, as a minority Government, from passing socialist measures; and the second was that, when the Labour Government was defeated, as sooner or later it was bound to be, the King would ask him to form a Government, as the leader of the only undefeated party in the House of Commons. He prepared, indeed, the ground for this position by insisting, in the speech in which he announced that he would ask his supporters to defeat Mr. Baldwin, that there was no automatic right in the Prime Minister to be granted a dissolution when he asked for it from the King; the latter, on the contrary, was the sole judge of when to grant that right in terms of the situation confronting the country.

In fact, King George V agreed to Mr. MacDonald's request for a dissolution without any difficulty; and it is now highly probable that this part of the royal prerogative is as obsolete as the royal veto power. It ought, indeed, to have been obvious to as skilful a constitutionalist as Mr. Asquith that, if the King had refused Mr. MacDonald's request, and asked the Liberal leader to form a Government, he, too, as the head of a minority party, would have been sooner or later defeated, and been compelled to ask for a dissolution. That would have put the King in the difficult and delicate position of giving to one Prime Minister a right he had denied to his predecessor; for the King could hardly have asked Mr. Baldwin to form a second government in a House of Commons which had already declared that it had no confidence in him and his colleagues. Nor is it easy to accept Mr. Asquith's view that by voting against Mr. Baldwin, he let in a Labour Government which he could always defeat if it attempted socialist measures. The first Labour Government did indeed fall upon an issue wholly unconnected with socialism. But if Mr. MacDonald, as Prime Minister, had been a man of foresight and courage, his best policy would have been to introduce a bold programme of socialist measures, challenge the Opposition to defeat him upon that programme, and, if defeated, have sought a general election in which the imaginative sweep of his proposals would have made a profound appeal to an electorate most of whom never grasped the technical niceties of the issue upon which he did dissolve, and did not see, in any of his measures save the Wheatley Housing Act, anything for which an ordinary Tory Government would not have been readily responsible.

Nor do I think that Professor Muir's use of the experience of the Social Democratic Government in Sweden is really valid. It is true that it was a minority Government, that it passed a number of useful measures, and that it saved Sweden from the grave unemployment which was the usual consequence of the first World War and the great depression. But, as Professor Muir himself says, "it practically dropped its theoretic doctrines", by which he really means that it ceased to behave like a Socialist Party in order not to be defeated in a Riksdag where it was in a minority. He talks of its "reasonable" measures, which

commanded the support of the whole country; but, concealed within those genial phrases, are the assumptions
that a party must follow public opinion, and not lead it,
and that it must make the other parties in the legislature
feel that they have an effective share in the management
of affairs. The real point of Professor Muir's argument
thus becomes a plea for "coalition measures" without a
Coalition Government; and what is "reasonable" is regarded as the abandonment of the central principles the
the party was founded to sustain. I venture to guess that
the true source of Professor Muir's satisfaction with
the Swedish situation was the existence there of three
well-entrenched parties, and a Government introducing
measures much on the lines of the Liberal Government of
1906 in Great Britain when few people foresaw how rapid
would be the decline of the Liberal Party.

V

THE PLACE OF THE BACK-BENCHER

Nothing in this must be taken to mean that there are not
important Parliamentary problems that it is urgent to try
and solve. All of them concern the place of the private
member in the House of Commons, and all of them are
not the less important for being, in no small part, concealed from the public view. The first is the need to
recognise that being a member of the House of Commons
is an onerous job, and that the lighter the burden can be
made the more effective is the member likely to be. For
the man with a large income outside his Parliamentary

salary, the work, indeed, does not present excessive difficulties. He can look after his constituency by keeping a paid agent there, by employing one or more secretaries to look after his correspondence, or to help him with the material he requires for his speeches. He can maintain a house in London, if he lives elsewhere, and a car, with, perhaps, a chauffeur, will solve all the problems he confronts as a result of late, or even all-night, sittings. He can pay his own election expenses, entertain his supporters on a scale that makes him popular, and subscribe enough to local organisations in his own constituency to make it a pretty difficult matter for a rival in his own party to get the nomination as candidate away from him once he has got reasonably well known in his division. He may be a peer's son, a big landowner, a successful manufacturer, a lawyer with a large practice, an expert in the collection of company directorships, or a journalist who, with three or four weekly articles in the daily or weekly press, either at home or abroad, may easily multiply by three or four the thousand pounds per annum that he receives as his Parliamentary salary, together with a first-class railway ticket to and from his constituency. I know well a Conservative member for a division less than fifty miles from London who told me, before the second World War, that he secured his nomination as candidate by offering the local association to spend not less than five thousand pounds a year in the constituency, and that, over a period of more than twelve years, he had in fact spent an annual average of round seven thousand pounds.

As a rule, every House contains a number of men in this secure financial position, and there will, of course, be more of them when a Tory, and not a Labour, Government is in power. But the member who has nothing but his Parliamentary salary to rely upon, has, especially if he is married, a hard problem to face. Unless he has a seat as safe as that of Mr. Shinwell at Seaham, or of Mr. James Griffiths at Llanelly, he will be unwise, unless he and his family live in London, to set up house there; he will do better to live in a hotel or in furnished rooms, or share with a group of other members a flat or a house of not too expensive a character. At best, he can share with two or three other members the part-time services of a secretary; normally, unless he is a trade-union member who can use the facilities of his office, he must write, and pay the postage for, all his letters himself; and a fairly average expenditure on letters and telephones will come to something like one hundred and thirty pounds each year. He will normally pay something to his constituency party, pay for his meals, entertain a little, even if moderately and infrequently, buy an occasional book, some periodicals, and make allowance for clothes, an occasional holiday, and the almost certain need for some moderate life insurance. It must be added that a not inconsiderable number of members have to get up material for their speeches, and that, despite the help given to them by the librarian and his staff at the House of Commons, this may well entail the expenditure of a good deal of time, especially when a member is tempted to look up what he needs to know while a debate is going on in the Chamber. It is, in fact, difficult to see how any M.P. who employs a secretary can, after he has paid the expenses he cannot avoid, have more than £300 per annum left out of his

salary for all expenses not directly connected with his
Parliamentary duties. If one compares that with Con-
gressional salaries and allowances in the American
Congress or the Canadian Parliament, it is clear that a
British member who has no other resources than his salary
is working within an impossible margin.

When, therefore, Sir Noel Arkell writes to *The Times*,
to insist that he has "much, much more confidence in an
M.P. who can afford to back his conscience with his vote",
he is really asking for membership of the House to be
confined to rich men only. On any showing, that would
be a misfortune of the first order. The House of Commons
needs not only the equivalent of the Office Building in
Washington, so that its members may write their letters
and interview their visitors in a decent privacy, but the
members need also adequate secretarial assistance, and
salaries large enough to make them independent of any
source of income except that derived from their own
exertions. Mr. Quintin Hogg, a Conservative M.P., suggested to the Select Committee an annual salary of
£1,500 plus obviously necessary expenses. If, in the latter,
there were included the salary of a well-trained secretary,
and free postage up to some such annual sum as £150,
I think the M.P. would be safeguarded against a number
of undesirable pressures to which recent evidence has
shown he is subject—payment for gossip to newspapers,
a weekly column in some Sunday journal, an anxiety to
broadcast as often as he can and, not least, his knowledge
that, if he gets on the wrong side of the party whips, he
may very easily find himself not only without a seat, but
also involved in debts that it may be very difficult for him

to pay. The member of Parliament is entitled to work under conditions where he does not feel that independence on some important issue may involve penalties not only upon himself, but, it may well be, upon his family as well.

To this must be added the fact that the Parliamentary organisation of his party ought to give him an effective chance to comment upon its policy before its leaders are so committed to it that any change in the policy they announce can be represented as the proof that they dare not stand up to their back-benchers. The present organisation of the Labour Party in the House of Commons is a good example of a freedom in appearance which, in fact, conceals a far too rigid control. There are no standing orders in the Parliamentary Party. It is generally expected that a member will follow his leaders when he receives a three-line whip; and it is virtually a conventional rule that, while a member may speak against his party where his conscience is involved, he will refrain from voting against it in the division lobby. The party has, when its leaders are in office, a Liaison Committee, with a paid and permanent secretary, which acts as the go-between in the relations between the Government and its supporters, and arranges the weekly meeting, during the Session, of the Parliamentary Party at which any business is discussed which either private members or Ministers desire to bring before it; and, in the normal way, the chairman of the Liaison Committee will arrange that any Minister particularly concerned in some discussion of which notice has been given will be present to explain, and, if necessary, to defend his policy. Once in each session, the National

Executive Committee of the Party is present at one of these meetings, though it is rare for anyone but its chairman to speak; and he usually confines himself to a brief expression of good wishes. The Parliamentary Party is also represented at the National Council of Labour—at which the Labour Party, the Trades Union Congress General Council, and the Co-operative Union seek to co-ordinate their work—and it is divided regionally and functionally into groups which discuss the special problems with which they are concerned. These groups have, from time to time, evolved policies which they have put before the appropriate Minister or Ministers; and they have, from time to time also, discussed policy, at the Ministerial level, when they had doubts about some attitude on which they desired clarification or change. On paper, this may seem to give the private member some real opportunity to speak his mind. In fact, the whole structure is really an elaborate façade behind which little that is effective really takes place. The meeting of the Parliamentary Party usually lasts for one hour in each week of the session, so that few of its members ever get the chance of serious speech, and the Minister, almost invariably, has the last word. The group committees of a regional nature largely, though not wholly, confine themselves to matters of an organisational character within the area that concerns them; and the functional groups, when they have positive proposals or important criticisms to make, usually find that the time-table of the House is fatal to the first, and the principle of collective Cabinet responsibility is fatal to the second. Ministers are usually willing to meet a deputation of members upon some special topic, but it usually takes something like the threat of a party revolt to cause them to change their minds; and too large a number of them fall back, in the face of criticism, upon that claim to loyalty as the alternative to dissolution which is usually enough to make the discussion end in some kind of harmony. There are occasions, indeed, when a Minister will explain in confidence to the Party meeting some vital change upon which the Cabinet has already decided—a kind of complimentary fore-knowledge which usually results in its easier passage on the floor of the House; and there was one famous occasion in this Parliament when an important group of members, unable, after long effort, to get any attention for their views, took the risk of putting down an amendment to the Address in reply to the King's Speech, and putting it to the test of a vote in the House.

But a direct challenge of this kind carries penalties with it which it is not easy to ask an ambitious young member to accept. The Prime Minister, not seldom with the advice of the Chief Whip, can usually break up an insurgent group by the offer of a place in the Government to one or more of its members who are known to be less inflexible than the others. He may allow it to become known that a constant critic can make up his mind that he cannot hope to be selected, not merely for office, but for the chance of being used in one of a score of opportunities, the delegation to the Assembly of the United Nations, for example, or that which goes to the European Assembly, membership in which brings him into public notice. The persistent critic may find himself not only frowned upon in the Parliamentary Party generally, but it is rarely difficult for the Prime Minister, or one of his half-dozen more important colleagues, to ask the National Executive Committee of the Party to put pressure on him; and that pressure can vary from the semi-official hint, perhaps in the form of a talk with, or a letter from, the Party's National Agent, that he may find it harder than he imagines to win renomination for his present seat at the next election, through a demand for specific assurances of loyalty, to the critic's actual expulsion from the Party. In the many years that I myself served on the Labour Party's National Executive Committee, I have never known a request for expulsion which won the support of the Party's leader in the House of Commons to be refused. It is certainly worth reflecting that the expulsion of Mr. Zilliacus, approved by an overwhelming majority of the Party's Annual Conference in 1949, was based on differences about foreign policy which, had the same rules applied in the Tory Party, would obviously have resulted in the exclusion of Mr. Churchill, to take one illustrious example only, from its ranks. Nor ought it to be forgotten that Sir Stafford Cripps, Mr. Aneurin Bevan, and Mr. George Strauss, all of whom were expelled from membership of the Party in 1939, are now amongst its Ministers of Cabinet rank, the first two of them being members of the Cabinet itself; and that Viscount Jowitt, since 1945 the Labour Government's Lord Chancellor, followed Mr. Ramsay MacDonald into the "National" Government in 1931, and only returned to the Labour Party when, after losing his seat in the General Election of that year, he discovered that the "National" Government had no special anxiety to make use of his services. The Labour Minister of Food, Mr. John Strachey, after being a Labour member of Parliament from 1929-31, was, for a brief period, a supporter of Sir Oswald Mosley in that "New Party" which preceded the formation of the Fascist Party, and, after breaking with him, was, until the Russo-German Pact of 1939, among the staunchest "fellow travellers" whom the Communist Party of Great Britain attracted to its support. Compared with any of these eminent men, I should myself have argued that Mr. D. N. Pritt, who was expelled in 1940, over a difference with the National Executive Committee about the Russo-Finnish War in which events proved him to be as obviously right as it proved the National Executive Committee to be obviously wrong, and Mr. Zilliacus, who was expelled in 1949, were clearly treated with an unjustifiable and disproportionate harshness.

Neither the Tory Party nor the Liberal Party has a discipline so rigid as that of the Labour Party; and it is difficult not to feel that, when the Labour Party is in office, it would benefit a good deal were it to make the practice of toleration as real as it seeks to persuade the public to believe it is. Most of the differences which lead to intolerance arise from three facts. First of all, the trade union element in the Party is, naturally enough in the light of its history, schooled to a continuity of obedience from its members which begins from the moment when, though discussion be short or long, a vote on the issue has been taken; and largely, though not wholly, it has imposed this standard of loyalty upon the Party it has done so much both to found and to sustain. The second

G

reason is that the Party leaders, when in office, take the view very strongly that their responsibility is to Parliament, as the Government, and not to the members of the Labour Party; though, therefore, there is consultation, this usually takes place after, and not before, the Government has made up its mind, and is largely ineffective for the simple reason that, especially since Mr. Churchill's sound and fury in the General Election of 1945, the Cabinet is very sensitive to a charge that it is yielding to pressure external to its own membership. The third reason is the important one that the peculiar composition of the Party's National Executive makes it, on all matters of doctrine, an instrument of the leaders in office which is incapable of effective independence; and it is only on the rarest occasions that an appeal from the National Executive to the Annual Conference will be successful, since overwhelming voting-power at the Conference is in the hands of the trade unions whose decision is shaped by the first of the three facts to which I have drawn attention.

I have said that, in the light of experience, there was every reason for a far closer co-operation between Ministers and the functional committees of the Parliamentary Labour Party I have just described. It gives the private member a genuine sense that he can, if he so desires, be useful, and that the effort he makes to understand some special topic of discussion is not likely to be thrown away merely because, on some special occasion, he has not been able to catch the Speaker's eye. I think it would be of real value if the National Executive Committee of the Party, instead of being limited, as now, to what is hardly as much as a formal relation to the Parliamentary Party, had regular monthly meetings with it to discuss matters of joint interest, and were thus given the chance, now absent for all serious purposes, of bringing to the notice of Ministers topics of interest upon which they were jointly agreed. The organisational weakness of the Labour Party, as compared with either the Tories or the Liberals, is that, mostly for historical reasons, the different ruling elements in it have scarcely any contact except upon the formal and official level. The result is that there is an absence of ease in their relationship; there is little of the "give and take" that comes from the casual habit of dining together, even of week-ending together, instead of depending upon a series of set meetings in which time is always frustrating a set agenda. This is true, for instance, of the relations between the Cabinet and the T.U.C. General Council, and also between this latter body and the Party's National Executive. Indeed, though the ideological gap between Labour and Mr. Churchill's Government was wider than between Labour and Mr. Attlee's Government, I should be tempted to judge that the relations between them in the first instance were easier than in the second because they were kept on a much less formal plane. And Mr. Churchill, as Prime Minister, gave the rank and file of the Parliamentary Party a much less profound sense of being kept at arm's length by encouraging them to bring him the result of discussions between the "official opposition" and the Tory 1922 Committee than has been the case since 1945. The discussions, as on the repeal of the Trade Disputes and Trade Unions Act of 1927, may well have proved more abortive under Mr. Churchill than they have been under his successor; but there was a more genial and easy approach in the earlier period than in the later. And there have certainly been occasions when a Labour delegation has visited one or another of Mr. Attlee's ministers on which the cold rigour of their reception has resembled nothing so much as the frigidity with which Count Brockdorff-Rantzau was received when, in 1919, he led the German delegation to Versailles to hear the proposed terms of the Treaty of Versailles, and felt the icy atmosphere so strongly that it became physically impossible for him to stand up in making his speech in reply.

To this, as I think, there must be added, with quite special emphasis, the unsatisfactory position to which the discussion of foreign affairs always seems to lead in the House of Commons. This is not, of course, a new development. Of the Liberal Cabinet of 1906, Mr. Lloyd George has written that "during the whole of those eight years when I was a member of the Cabinet, I can recall no such review of the European situation being given to us as that which Sir Edward Grey delivered to the Colonial Conference in 1907, or to the Prime Ministers of the Dominions at the Committee of Imperial Defence in 1911. Even there, the information that was withheld was more important than that which was imparted. Direct questions were always answered with civility, but were not encouraged. We were made to feel that, in these matters, we were reaching our hands to the mysteries and we were too young in the priesthood to enter into the sanctuary reserved for the elect . . . As a matter of fact, we were hardly qualified to express any opinion on so important a matter, for we were not privileged to know any more of the essential facts than those which the ordinary newspaper reader could gather from the perusal of his morning journal ... What mattered just as much, perhaps even more, were the secret arrangements arrived at between the military and naval staffs of Britain, France, and Russia, as to the part their respective forces were to play in the event of war with Germany. None of those vital communications were placed at the disposal of the Cabinet. They were passed on to the Prime Minister and perhaps to one or two other Ministers. The rest of us were kept in the dark and were therefore not in a position to assess the realities of the foreign situation." [1] It is obvious that if this was the position of a Cabinet Minister who, after 1908, was certainly among the first four members of importance in Mr. Asquith's Government, it was very likely that the ordinary member of the House of Commons was in a still less favourable position to form a judgment.

I think it would be difficult to argue that the situation has, in this respect, greatly improved since Mr. Lloyd George wrote. It is, no doubt, true that there are many more members who have first-hand, and even close, acquaintance with foreign countries that come into the news; but, in such cases, if the private member cannot visit them at his own expense, it is more than likely that any evidence he presents in support of his views will be discounted, if it does not coincide with the outlook of the Foreign Secretary, on the ground that his expenses have been paid on his behalf by the Government of the country he has visited. It is to be expected that, in war-time, the Cabinet should give most of the support asked of it by

[1] *War Memoirs* (London, Odhams Ltd.), pp. 24–9.

the Prime Minister, and that the latter, in his turn, should often make speedy decisions to the outcome of which he has sometimes given insufficient consideration. It is pretty clear that this was the case with the now notorious acceptance both by Mr. Churchill and his Cabinet of the Roosevelt formula—itself a half-remembered inspiration from a theme of the American Civil War—of "unconditional surrender". It is not easy to believe that the House of Commons has been honestly informed of the facts which have led to its approval of policies which have concerned grave issues like those of Abyssinia, Spain, Italy, Greece, Germany and Russia; and, not without skill, it has been manœuvred into something like an organised silence over the atomic bomb and the present state of our military commitments. On Spain, indeed, Mr. Eden maintained for many months what seemed so like an injured innocence of charges that the Nazis and the Fascists were using it as a theatre of preliminary operations that the Non-Intervention Committee which was so largely sponsored by Great Britain almost ceased to be a device of dishonesty even to those who were convinced that this was its purpose. It is doubtful whether a dozen members of the House realised that the policy of "unconditional surrender" meant a senseless struggle for Sicily which, in its turn, probably gave the Germans the time to prepare their long-drawn-out and costly rear-guard action in Italy itself. The critics of the Churchill Government at the Labour Party Conference of December 1944, of whom the principal was Mr. Aneurin Bevan, know by now that Mr. Churchill and Mr. Eden, having successfully deceived their Labour colleagues in the Coalition Government, left them in charge of a *damnosa hereditas* in which they were driven to continue the deception mainly because Mr. Ernest Bevin, who gave them the official Cabinet answer in 1944, had been misled into a complete misunderstanding of the whole problem.

That is hardly less true of Germany since its surrender in the spring of 1945. I do not think that the members of the Labour Party who so steadfastly supported Mr. Bevin's policy there would have done so at any rate with the vigour they did had they known that his pledge to nationalise the heavy industries of the Ruhr was one he never even attempted to enforce, and that the West German Republic he assisted in creating would presently come to be regarded by the United States as a major pillar in the bastion the United States was erecting in its "cold war" against the Soviet Union, into which, quite largely, he was led by seeing the problem of Russia rather through American eyes than through his own. In the General Election of 1945, the Labour Party pledged itself, if it was returned to power, to make every effort it could to maintain friendly relations with the Soviet Union. The British Government could fairly claim that Russia has done most of what it could to place obstacles in the way of those friendly relations; yet that does not explain why the effort to achieve them was so incomplete and brief, and why, under the leadership of Mr. Winston Churchill, Mr. Ernest Bevin was so ready to shape his policy to fit the effort of the United States to drive Russia into a position where its natural desire for security against an *Einkreisung* sponsored by American diplomacy should lead the world to the brink of a third World War. Nor does it explain the intense secrecy with which the British Government has surrounded its atomic energy policy, a secrecy of which the result has been to make Great Britain the ardent sponsor of the American plan for the control of atomic energy, even after the Russian discovery of the bomb had not only made that plan entirely obsolete, but had gone far towards making it certain that, were war to come in atomic form, the very survival of Great Britain would be in jeopardy.

I have limited my illustrations of the great weakness in Parliament before a secretive Cabinet to a small number of instances. I have not included the incredible muddle Mr. Ernest Bevin has made in the Middle East, by accepting, in the face of the quite specific pledges of the Labour Party Conference, the advice of his supposed "experts" in the Foreign Office, despite both the shame and the failure in which it has involved him in the state which is now Israel. Nor have I dwelt, as it is tempting to dwell, upon the mystery of Anglo-Spanish relations which, despite the public withdrawal of our Ambassador from Madrid in response to a strong resolution passed by the Assembly of the United Nations, have pursued a hidden existence of their own the probable outcome of which will be restoration to Spain both of diplomatic recognition and assistance, both military and economic, which Great Britain will then support on the ground that it cannot be out of step with a policy in which the United States will lead, since the geographical position of Spain makes it one of the vital points in the control of the Mediterranean. In all this, I am concerned much more with the implications of the point hammered in by Mr.

Lloyd George, and still as true as when he made it nearly a generation ago, that if necessary information is withheld from most members of the Cabinet, how few are the members of the House of Commons in a position to penetrate the thick veil of secrecy which is cast round all the vital steps which are being taken in international relations, and for which mainly the usually *a posteriori* support of the House of Commons is sought. In our own day, perhaps, the frenzy of enthusiasm with which the Munich Pact was accepted in 1938 is the supreme example of support through ignorance. There are few members of the House, Mr. Churchill very notably apart, who can look back on that debate without feeling a deep sense of humiliation at the ease with which it was misled.

It is far from easy to see a remedy proportionate to the disease. A body like the Senate Committee on Foreign Relations in the United States would not suit our situation, since the key to its authority, and to that of its subcommittees, lies in that separation of powers which is alien from the natural design of Parliamentary constitutions. Nor, I believe, should we find what we want in the parallel Foreign Affairs Commission of the French Chamber, the power of which resides mainly in the fact that the multiplicity of parties there rarely enables any Government to dominate its composition; and the right of the commission to interfere with the Foreign Minister's decision is largely minimised by the high probability that his defeat will not cause a dissolution of the Chamber. The most available safeguards for our position appear to be two. The first is the assurance that the collective responsibility of the Cabinet will be made real in this realm;

and that, accordingly, it will cease to be within the power of three or four members to take action of which the remainder are in ignorance until its results become a matter of public knowledge. The second is the creation, so often urged by Ministers in opposition, and repudiated by them when in office, of an advisory committee of the House of Commons on foreign affairs, which will sit privately, but regularly, and have the power to summon before it the Secretary of State, if he does not normally attend, or, in his absence abroad, one of his two Parliamentary subordinates, while on occasions of exceptional importance it ought to have access to the Prime Minister and the Minister of Defence. It should be able, further, to call for the assistance of Ambassadors, permanent officials, and the heads of Defence Commands abroad, where their evidence seems vital to a judgment it needs to form; given the present ease of communication by air, this does not, I think, present any insuperable difficulty about time.

I assume, of course, that an advisory Foreign Affairs Committee of this kind would not publish such comments as it might choose to make, but communicate them to the Prime Minister whose duty it would be to circulate them, with such comments as he wished to make, to the members of the Cabinet. If it is said in criticism of this proposal that it might weaken the Minister's responsibility for policy, or that it might slow down the speed of the decisions he has to make, the answers, I conceive, are simple ones. Ministerial responsibility developed in order that the Minister might be called to account by Parliament, and not in order that, where he so desires, he may evade his control. Where speed of decision is necessary, no Minister who thinks he can justify his action will hesitate to act swiftly; it is when he is doubtful of his own course, or still more, is being urged, by the zeal of his officials, on to some special journey about which he is not wholly convinced, that he is likely to take time for consideration; and it is precisely in such cases as these that the value of consultation with his Advisory Committee becomes outstanding. It has, I think, the further merits, first, that it makes the Prime Minister's interest in the work of the Foreign Office continuous, and important to his own political fortunes, and, secondly, that it gives us as good an assurance as we can ask for that, in this urgent realm of effort, the collective responsibility of the Cabinet is real, and not a mask for the ignorance of all but the few whom the Prime Minister is ready to take into his confidence. It is always worth remembering that most of the Asquith Cabinet did not know of the conversations between the British and French Staffs, which his predecessor, Sir Henry Campbell-Bannerman, had authorised in 1905, until Mr. Asquith himself answered a question on the subject put to him from the front Opposition bench by Lord Quickswood, then Lord Hugh Cecil. On this type of Parliamentary control, I add that it seems to me important to establish similar machinery for the oversight of policy in the Colonial Office. Both of the realms of decision have the special characteristic, which does not hold in the domestic realm, that Parliamentary control over each of them is, in the absence of such institutions, largely unreal because there is no continuous scrutiny of a relation which mainly consists of interchanges, direct and indirect, between the Minister

and his officials. I see no reason why, under suitable safeguards, we should not make the House of Commons
something more than a rubber stamp confirming policies
of which it knows little or nothing until it is too late to
alter them at all, or refusing confirmation at the cost,
which a party with a majority is rarely willing to pay, of
forcing the Prime Minister to seek a dissolution of
Parliament.

VI

PARLIAMENTARY CONTROL OF THE
NATIONALISED INDUSTRIES

There is one final aspect of Parliamentary activity about
which some careful thinking is desirable. Since 1945, to
the already publicly owned and operated postal, tele-
graph, and telephone services, the Government has added
the public ownership of the Bank of England, together
with that of six other industries. The steel industry has
already been nationalised, though the fulfilment of the
Act will depend upon whether the Labour Party is given
a second lease of power. It is widely agreed that the day-
to-day operation of these industries should remain in the
hands of the Boards of these Public Corporations, with
responsibility to the Minister only for the general framework of policy within which he orders the Corporation to
work subject only to the overriding will of Parliament.
That overriding will, apart from any special vote of
censure, has come to mean a debate in each year on the
Annual Report of the Board to the Minister who is

responsible for its working, and, in a general way, those debates have been workmanlike and illuminating. But there still remain, in this procedure, two difficulties which, sooner or later, the House of Commons will have to face. The first is the doubt whether one day spent on the annual report of a great industry, which means seven hours out of which the Front Bench speakers will take about three hours, leaves the ordinary members, some of whom can speak on the industry with a direct experience of its working, sufficient time to make their views known about its policies. The second is the problem of just what is going to happen when, instead of six publicly owned industries, there are sixteen or twenty or even twenty-five; a dozen years from now what I speak of as a future may well have become an actual problem. It would, I believe, be unfortunate if these reports were relegated to the position of the Estimates of a Government Department—were, that is to say, discussed only when any of them led the Opposition to ask that time be set apart for their examination. It is, I think, of high importance that an industry in public hands should, not less for reasons of psychology and morale than on economic grounds, be made aware that it will be subject to close scrutiny in the House of Commons. That puts both the Minister and the members of his Boards into the proper mood of watchfulness where they can prove that their expenditure has been sensible, and that they have not allowed the desire to show a surplus at the end of the year to interfere with desirable experiment, not least with technological experiment.

To achieve these two aims, I should like to see set up a series of Standing Committees in the House of Commons, one for each of the industries concerned. The appropriate Minister should then send the Report he has received from the Board of the Industry to the relevant Committee, which should spend such time in examining its contents as it deems necessary to satisfy itself that its exploration has been a thorough one; the exploration should, generally, be in private, and resemble rather the proceedings of a Select Committee than of a debate in the House of Commons. I should give to each of these Committees a small but highly expert secretariat, which could draw attention to matters calling either for praise or blame, and would draw its attention, also, to matters connected with the Report upon which it would have been desirable that comment should have been made. I should give the Committee the power to summon the Minister before it, and also the chairman of the National Board of the industry concerned; and, with the Minister's consent, the chairman of any Regional Board in the industry whose evidence seemed likely to have value in the context of the examination. I think that the Committee, also, should be empowered to receive evidence in writing, and, if it thought fit, to summon as a witness for examination anyone whose written evidence seemed to suggest the value of an oral hearing. When this process had been completed, I should expect the Committee to report to the House of Commons, with the right always inherent in one or more of its members to publish a minority report. A procedure of this kind would give us at least three important assurances. It would make the Parliamentary control of the industry more than a formality, in the same way that we have seen, in recent years, that the work of the Committee on Privileges makes the power of the House either to protect, or to correct, its members a very real thing. It would create interest in the industry among the public, so that the voters would come to appreciate its successes and its failures. Not least, it would be almost as strong a safeguard as we could create against the danger that a publicly owned industry, which does not have to answer to the House of Commons for its day-to-day work, would slip into those bureaucratic habits which may easily become endemic in all large-scale enterprises, whether nationally or privately owned. Here I mean by "bureaucratic habits" those temptations, always so attractive to a busy man, to apply a rule or regulation that has seemed to work well previously to a situation which is superficially analogous, though close examination would prove that the differences in the situation are far more important than its likeness to the old; and to these temptations must be added the further one, that only the devil himself could have invented, of asking one's subordinates to provide, at the cost of great energy and time, a mass of complicated information which, when collected, is never put to any future use.

VII

CONCLUSION

On the House of Commons as an institution I would like to add this final word. With all the changes that have taken place in it during this last half-century, I see no decline in its greatness, nor any ultimate danger that it should be by-passed in its fundamental purposes, above all in the most fundamental of all its purposes, the duty to see that the conditions are maintained which protect the freedom of the ordinary citizen. I do not accept Mr. Amery's[1] view that Parliament is threatened either by bodies like a party's executive committee, or by outside organisations like the Federation of British Industries or the Trades Union Congress. I do not accept, either, his fear that majority rule will be abused, and the historic traditions of our constitution broken by the use of angry misconceptions of what those traditions imply. On the contrary, I should argue that, in the years since 1945, public respect for the House of Commons has grown swiftly, and is much deeper today than it was either in 1925 or in 1935. Mr. Amery himself has noted that it is accepted by Labour Ministers as much as by Conservative, and that a Labour Party Conference is permeated by the characteristics of what is best in the Parliamentary system no less than the conferences of the older parties. I see no danger to the supremacy of the House of Commons in the new phase of its long life upon which it has entered. If there is a danger ahead, it seems to me to lie in the use of great financial and industrial power to prevent the will of the electorate being made effective by the Government of its choice. That is a risk to which Mr. Herbert Morrison[2] has recently and vigorously drawn attention. In a period of rapid social change, it is a risk that might easily become

[1] *Thoughts on the Constitution* (Oxford ed. of 1945). Mr. Amery does not mention the F.B.I. but speaks only of "the danger of irresponsible power" in the Trades Union Congress, p. 45.

[2] Speech of 26th November 1949.

a grave one; for it represents the effort of men who, though small in numbers, have the immense powers great wealth confers, to challenge, by means outside the ordinary conventions of Parliamentary life, the right of the House of Commons to support the Government of the day, and put its measures upon the Statute Book. That is the method which invites all parties to a disrespect for constitutional tradition. If we can overcome this risk we may be able to make the social and economic changes our national life requires while retaining the unity of a commonwealth that can live at peace with itself. In the light of history, it is difficult to imagine a more splendid achievement.

PART TWO

THE CABINET

VIII

THE CABINET AND THE PRIME MINISTER

THE immense growth in the authority of the Cabinet in the first half of the twentieth century is, in many ways, the most striking aspect of constitutional change in this period. It has, of course, been greatly assisted by the impact of two world wars, in each of which the centralisation of power in its hands was an inevitable concomitant of organisation for victory, and this centralisation was, in its turn, strengthened by the fact that in each of the conflicts, the Prime Minister became, in the first case just after two years, and in the second just after nine months, almost a dictator by consent upon whose leadership the general character of the war effort came to depend. It is unquestionable that a large part of the Cabinet's power is the outcome of a relative decline in the authority of Parliament. This is due, in considerable degree, to the far greater range and complexity of the problems the solutions of which the Cabinet places before Parliament for acceptance; and in a considerable degree, also, to the increasing authority of party organisation over its supporters, both Labour and Tory, in the House of Commons. Since 1916, indeed, when the Liberal Party split over the accession of Mr. Lloyd George to the Premiership, no Liberal organisation has ever been able to exercise any effective control over any of its members who chooses to take a line of his own; but, before the Liberal split, the party machine was as influential in its power over Liberal members in the House as the machines of the rival parties.

But the growth of Cabinet power has not meant the reduction of the House of Commons to what may be termed colonial status. If it is true to say that the general direction of the House is determined by the Cabinet, it is equally true to say that the authority of the Cabinet is always tempered by the knowledge that any grave error on its part in estimating what the House of Commons is prepared to accept, may lead to its defeat, or its need to give way, or the elimination of a Minister who cannot maintain his authority there. It was the House of Commons which put the seal of an ignominious end upon the Balfour Cabinet of 1905; and it was the House of Commons which broke the Chamberlain Government in May 1940. No doubt, in each case, the verdict of the House was reinforced by the clear proof of a strong public feeling outside; but that public feeling is always a factor in determining the breaking-point of members' loyalty to the Cabinet they normally support. So, again, it is reasonable to conclude that it was in large degree foreknowledge of what the Commons would demand which made the Trades Disputes Act of 1906 so much wider in scope than the first thought of the Liberal Government, as it was the drive of the back-benchers, after the Lords' rejection of the Budget in 1909, which drove the Asquith Government

to fight so firmly for the curtailment of the power of
the upper chamber which seemed to the generation of
1913 almost as epoch-making a change as that of 1832.
There are innumerable examples of the House making it
inevitable that a Minister should accept changes in a
measure the outlines of which had seemed rigidly drawn
when it was first introduced; and the famous sacrifice of
Sir Samuel Hoare (now Lord Templewood) on the altar
of the House's indignation at the Hoare–Laval Treaty
shows clearly that, if the Cabinet is normally the master
of the House of Commons, there are always limits to its
mastery of which it must take account.

The Cabinet remains, in essence, a committee of the
party or parties with a majority in the House of Commons. It is true that the Ministers of the Crown Act, 1937,
limits the number of Ministers who can sit in the House
of Commons, and thus ensures that some shall sit in the
House of Lords; and it is important to recognise that a
Prime Minister of any character has a pretty wide discretion in the choice of its members, especially in Cabinets
formed, or reformed, during a period of war. Many of
his choices, no doubt, are obvious; the history of how Mr.
Arthur Henderson became Foreign Secretary in 1929
shows that in a party Government a vital member of the
party can always set limits to the discretion a Prime
Minister can exercise. Nevertheless, that discretion is both
wide and mysterious. Despite the reasons he has himself
offered us in his *War Memoirs*, some of Mr. Lloyd
George's choices are not easy to understand. The selection, by Mr. Ramsay MacDonald, of Lord Chelmsford to
be his First Lord of the Admiralty in 1924 remains with-

out real clarification in the light of their slight acquaintance. We have still to learn how it was that Mr. Churchill
decided to invite Lord Leathers, who had neither Parliamentary nor political experience, to sit in his War Cabinet;
and the reason for the brief appearance of Lord Inman in
Mr. Attlee's Government has, thus far, remained a well-
kept secret. Sir John Anderson's choice as Home Secretary
was, like his nomination to the Governorship of Bengal,
usually attributed to his great abilities as an administrator,
abilities which all his colleagues, both Parliamentary and
official, have united to praise. As a Minister in the House
of Commons he has hardly been in any way exceptional;
and though he calls himself a "National" member to
indicate his claim to be regarded as detached from party
conflict, neither his speeches nor the record of his votes
suggest that he seriously differs from the Tories in any
matters of real importance. What, therefore, makes his
direct nomination to the Cabinet a notable thing is the
fact that he is one of the rare cases of an outstanding civil
servant moving directly, after his relatively brief period
in India, to the political headship of a Ministry in which
he had once been Permanent Secretary. There is hardly
an analogous case to his, since, in 1903, Mr. (later Earl)
Balfour offered the Secretaryship of State for War to that
mysterious *éminence grise*, the late Viscount Esher; though
in Esher's case, the part he had played in army reform,
and his great personal influence with Edward VII, were
no doubt a large part of the explanation why Mr. Balfour
was so anxious to secure his services in the Cabinet. Lord
Milner, when he joined the Lloyd George Government
in 1917, was already one of the three or four outstanding

Conservative leaders in the House of Lords; and Field-Marshal Smuts combined a great Dominion position with remarkable abilities, Mr. Lloyd George's use of which in the Cabinet of the first World War is a remarkable instance of the imaginative insight that great Welshman brought to the exercise of the Prime Minister's power of choice.

Even apart from these special cases the Prime Minister's choice of his colleagues in his Cabinet has remained largely a matter of his own discretion, though, periods of coalition apart, he has usually worked within the framework of his party. In general it remains true that there are some half-dozen colleagues whom he thinks it essential to include, that there is another half-dozen his choice of whom is likely to be justified by their performance after they have taken office, and that the remainder might easily have been replaced by other members of their party without the ordinary citizen noticing that the character of the Cabinet has been significantly changed. Few people now remember names like those of Mr. (later Lord) Bridgeman, or Sir John Gilmour, Sir Robert (later Viscount) Horne, Mr. Tom Shaw, or Mr. Vernon Hartshorn, though all of them enjoyed, after 1919, and before 1929, their brief span of glory in attaining that Cabinet rank which is the objective of every ambitious politician; Sir Robert Horne was even Chancellor of the Exchequer in Mr. Baldwin's first Government, and only dropped out of office when, in 1925, Mr. Baldwin offered the Exchequer to Mr. Churchill and sought to persuade Sir Robert Horne to go to the Ministry of Labour. Sir Robert thought his acceptance of the Ministry of Labour

would be a blow to his dignity and prestige, and he preferred to play the part of the "candid friend" in the first
months of the Baldwin Administration, believing that it
would be but a short time before the Prime Minister
would find it imperative to offer him some post proportionate to his own estimate of his claims. In fact, he never
again played any part of significance in politics. It requires,
in fact, an exceptional situation or a man of outstanding
ability to enter into a conflict with the Prime Minister
with any hope of victory; an important cabal within his
party may do so, but, for the most part, the Prime
Minister is as powerful as he wishes to be as long as he
plays his hand with reasonable care. Palmerston had his
famous "tit-for-tat" with Lord John Russell in the year
after his chief dismissed him from the office of Foreign
Secretary; but he owed a great deal not only to the international situation, but also to his emphatic independence
of Queen Victoria and the Prince Consort to whose
wishes Lord John Russell was supposed to be excessively
deferential. Lord Salisbury broke the career of Lord
Randolph Churchill almost without effort. Mr. Joseph
Chamberlain sought in vain to impose his ideas upon Mr.
Arthur Balfour. Once Sir Henry Campbell-Bannerman
had accepted the royal invitation to form a Government
in 1905, he had no difficulty in breaking up the agreement
of Mr. Asquith, Sir Edward Grey and Mr. Haldane to
force him to go to the Lords as the condition upon which
alone they would take office under him. The dislike for
Mr. Churchill which led Mr. Ramsay MacDonald to
exclude him from the "National" Government of 1931
would, almost certainly, have left him a permanent

back-bencher for the rest of his political career had the policy of "appeasement" been a success; and it is worth remarking that, when Mr. Eden resigned from the Chamberlain Government when the Prime Minister decided to make peace with Mussolini on the latter's own terms, only Viscount Cranborne (now Lord Salisbury) followed his example; and that no single Minister, a few months later, after the shameless cynicism of Munich, dreamed of following Sir Alfred Duff Cooper's determination to dissociate himself from the disastrous document which Mr. Neville Chamberlain so curiously regarded as a striking victory.

On the other hand, it has usually taken a pretty tough conspiracy to get a Prime Minister to surrender his leadership. Up to the very day before his fall, Mr. Asquith was quite confident that he had defeated Mr. Lloyd George's intrigues to make him a minor figure in his own Cabinet; and he resigned in almost serene confidence that he would prove so indispensable that only brief discussion would ensue before he resumed his Premiership on his own terms. He found, on the contrary, that the nimble intrigues by which Lord Beaverbrook had wedded Mr. Bonar Law to Mr. Lloyd George were fatal to the strategy he had conceived; and he was overwhelmed when men upon whose support he was confident he could rely accepted office in the Cabinet, which Mr. Lloyd George was commissioned to form on Mr. Bonar Law's advice, without any hesitation. Others, like Mr. E. S. Montagu and Mr. Winston Churchill, accepted office under the new Prime Minister a few months later; and, too proud to serve under one whom he had commanded, Mr.

Asquith never held office again. When, moreover, the then Tory Chief Whip, Sir George Younger, decided in 1922 that Mr. Lloyd George's value to his party was ended, he would not have been able to break the Coalition, even with its immense Tory majority, if Mr. Bonar Law, then in semi-retirement, had not made a dramatic reappearance on the side of Younger, and used his authority, and that mask of selflessness which, in fact, concealed a profound ambition for power, to outweigh the influence of men as powerful in Tory councils as Lord Birkenhead and Sir Austen Chamberlain. In 1931, of course, Mr. Ramsay MacDonald was only made Prime Minister as a stratagem to confuse and divide both the Labour Party and the electorate; if his position gave him influence, the real power, until the moment of his resignation, was always in Mr. Baldwin's hands. Mr. Neville Chamberlain had no difficulty in keeping his hold upon the Premiership until the Narvik debate. After it, the dependence of national unity upon the formation of a Coalition into which the Labour and Liberal Parties would enter having become plain, Mr. Chamberlain made two urgent but futile efforts to secure the support of the Labour Party, but on each occasion his offer was unanimously refused. According to Mr. Churchill, he then sought to persuade Lord Halifax to be summoned by the King to succeed him as Prime Minister; and Mr. Churchill has told us that it was because Lord Halifax saw at once, with characteristic magnanimity, that a War Prime Minister must be in the Commons, that Mr. Chamberlain then tendered his advice to the King to send for Mr. Churchill. Here, certainly, there is a gap in Mr. Churchill's narrative, since some hours before Mr. Chamberlain's resignation, he had been informed by Mr. Attlee, on behalf of the Labour Party, that they would accept no leader of any Coalition they were invited to enter except Mr. Churchill himself; and they only accepted the continued presence of the "men of Munich" in the new Cabinet on Mr. Churchill's own urgent insistence that his position in the Tory Party would be impossible if Mr. Chamberlain and Lord Halifax were, with Viscount Simon, excluded from the Administration.

It is, however, obvious that a Prime Minister who knows how to play his cards well, and retains popularity with the rank and file of his party in the House of Commons, has an impregnable position in the Cabinet over which he presides. He appoints Ministers and can exact their resignation; it would require a combination of several Ministers against him, of the highest standing in the party, to defeat his exercise of this immense power. It is said that when, during the second World War, Mr. Churchill was Prime Minister there was at least one important occasion when a colleague of great prominence tried to limit his authority, much as Mr. Lloyd George tried to limit that of Mr. Asquith in 1916, by getting a number of important colleagues to join with him in insisting on changes in Cabinet policy. When he failed to find any supporters, he gave up the effort as impossible. When Mr. Attlee made a considerable alteration in his Cabinet in the autumn of 1947, he acted solely on his own initiative; if he had consultations with any of his more intimate colleagues, they were certainly on a personal level only, for I spent some hours that day with one of

Mr. Attlee's Ministers who, in the course of that time, was rung up on the telephone by four of his colleagues to ask him whether he had any news of the Prime Minister's decision about their future.

The Prime Minister has also the right to ask the King for a dissolution of Parliament, and it appears now beyond doubt that he will be granted the dissolution automatically, and that he need not consult his Cabinet upon the matter. The second of these developments is fairly new. Mr. MacDonald, according to Mr. Clynes, consulted his Cabinet about the dissolution of 1924; but Mr. Baldwin did not consult his colleagues over that of 1935. The spectacle of some of Mr. Attlee's colleagues urging him, both in public speeches and in obviously inspired articles in the press, to dissolve as soon as possible in the last few months of 1949, and of the Prime Minister stolidly keeping his own counsel, suggests that the right is personal in his office. Obviously, if he refuses to consult, his failure might easily jeopardise his position as leader of his party; I remember Snowden's conviction, after MacDonald's defeat in 1924, that it was Arthur Henderson's duty to stand against MacDonald for the leadership at the beginning of the session of 1925, and his angry prediction, when Henderson refused to do so, that it was only a question of time before MacDonald would lead the Labour Party to its ruin; a prediction amply fulfilled, though with the unexpected co-operation of Snowden, in 1931. The grant by the King of the right to dissolution has become automatic for the simple reason that, where this refusal resulted in the resignation of the Prime Minister, the King would be driven to grant it to his successor, and thus to depart from the neutrality that is the supreme characteristic of his position.

The Prime Minister has also the control of the agenda for each Cabinet meeting. Ever since the institution of the Cabinet secretariat, at the end of 1916, each Minister sends round to the Secretariat both the papers he desires to have circulated and any items he may wish to have placed on the Cabinet agenda. The Secretary to the Cabinet then draws up a provisional plan which has to be approved or amended by the Prime Minister. Since, persuasion apart, the agenda approved by the Prime Minister is final in the sense that the only other argument a disappointed colleague has, when his item is omitted, is resignation, and since there are few Ministers who desire to take the risk of its being accepted, a Prime Minister with a will of his own has the same power over the business of the Cabinet, as the Cabinet, in its turn, has over the business of the House. To this must be added that, if he so wishes, he can exercise a general oversight of all Departments; and the student of Mr. Churchill's second volume on the war of 1939 will note there a remarkable and fascinating commentary on the range of business which came under his direct observation. He is also the chairman of the Defence Committee, which means that, where he is interested in these questions and is not himself the Minister of Defence, his authority in this field will be paramount, and therefore the Chiefs of Staff Committee—now by far the most important organ in the Services—will inevitably assume that they must shape their plans to fit in with the preferences he indicates. And while the position of Foreign Secretary remains, under all circumstances, an important one, it is nevertheless always true that a Foreign Secretary must work under what it is difficult not to call the direct supervision of the Prime Minister; and we have had, since 1916, at least four Prime Ministers who were, in all matters of decisive importance, their own Foreign Secretaries; that was true of Mr. Lloyd George, of Mr. Ramsay Mac-Donald in his first Government, Mr. Neville Chamberlain, and Mr. Winston Churchill. And though Mr. Attlee has, in general, given Mr. Bevin a wide area of international policy upon which to fix his own outlook, there have been fields like India, and the international control of atomic energy, in which Mr. Attlee's own personal initiative has been the guiding factor in making decisions. I would venture the guess that even in other realms—though, with typical reserve, he has never ostentatiously thrust himself into the foreground—there have been decisions of major import in which, whoever has been the spokesman of the Foreign Office, the directive was given to him by Mr. Attlee; and I suspect that his directives have been continuous and fundamental when the effort to reach Commonwealth unity has been an element of high significance. We must remember, too, that it is the Prime Minister who decides to whom shall go the circulation of fundamental papers in foreign policy and the defence measures which so largely depend upon them.

It must not, either, be forgotten that the Prime Minister disposes of a large amount of patronage, in using which he need only consult the King's pleasure. Not only does he appoint all the members of the Government, now something like eighty posts. He chooses the Law Lords and the Lord Justices of Appeal; he chooses the two Archbishops, and all other members of the episcopal bench; his is the final voice in appointing the permanent heads of all Government Departments; he nominates the Provost of Eton, the Dean of Christ Church, and all the Regius Professors in the two ancient universities, as well as the Master of Trinity College, Cambridge; and, in this last instance, admirable as are the qualities of Mr. G. M. Trevelyan, I make bold to say that, since the choice of a successor to the great physicist J. J. Thomson fell to Mr. Churchill, it was fortunate for Mr. Trevelyan that he was a Harrow man. The Prime Minister, moreover, must be consulted about the choice of all important Ambassadors and Governors of colonies; how decisive his judgment may be in this matter is well illustrated by the bold steps Mr. Attlee took when, within a brief time after taking office, he recalled Lord Wavell from the Viceroyalty of India and, to the surprise of the world, sent out Lord Mountbatten to become, with so much distinction and insight, the last of a mighty succession, few names in which have not had some special weight in our imperial history. He nominates, also, the three Chiefs of Staff in the Defence Services, and I venture again to emphasise that, in his capacity as chairman of the Defence Committee, their first loyalty in their collective character as the Chiefs of Staff Committee is, inevitably and naturally, owed to him. Apart, finally, from the Order of Merit and the Order of the Garter in which, by a recent agreement between the King and the Prime Minister, nomination is to rest in the King's hands, he makes all recommendations connected with the Birthday and New Year Honours, as well as in any exceptional list for which he may ask approval.

No doubt this volume of patronage is small compared to that of which the President of the United States disposes; but, unlike the President, the Prime Minister has not to cope with any equivalent of Senatorial approval or Senatorial courtesy. He has hardly ever to consider the impact of public opinion; for, amid the many extraordinary choices Prime Ministers have made since 1906, only one has caused any angry expression of dissent, and the person involved made the problem of the Prime Minister concerned a simple one by refusing to accept the honour that had been offered to him. Otherwise, it has been rare indeed, in the last forty years, for the Prime Minister to encounter any difficulty over his patronage. When, therefore, it is remembered that, in eight years, Mr. Asquith recommended the creation of 115 peers, and Mr. Lloyd George 108 in slightly less than six years of this great office, the ability it implies to secure an almost personal loyalty in a number of vital professions, as well as in most classes of society, is obvious. From time to time, the Annual Conference of the Labour Party has passed resolutions against the acceptance by its members of hereditary titles, knighthoods and the like; in actual practice, from the general secretaries of the great trade unions down to some popular official in a local Labour Party, the satisfaction of appearing in the Honours list does not seem very different from the emotions aroused in members of the older parties. This will not seem surprising to anyone aware of the eagerness for decorations in the Soviet Union, though in the Russian case their possession is often accompanied by substantial privileges. It is not, therefore, surprising that the power of the Prime Minister's

patronage, though obscure in its results, is, nevertheless, a factor which helps to increase the formidable
authority its status would confer upon him on other
grounds.

This does not mean for one moment that the Prime
Minister enjoys an unchanging status. The dynamic of the
office, at any given moment, depends a good deal upon
the character of the man who holds it. Both Mr. Lloyd
George and Mr. Churchill appeared to dominate all their
colleagues, though it must be added that each of them
enormously enjoyed the dramatic exhibition of his authority, and was helped by the fact that his chief colleague felt
it an essential part of his function to leave to his chief the
role of prima donna on the public stage. Mr. Asquith and
Mr. Baldwin were, relatively, phlegmatic Prime Ministers, content to let their colleagues go their own way so
long as the safety of the Cabinet did not seem in jeopardy;
but Mr. Asquith showed, both in the crisis over the House
of Lords in 1909–11, and over the mutiny at the Curragh
in 1914, that he had a reserve of energy he could call into
play when the subject-matter of the problem really
gripped him. Nor is it, I think, unfair to say that, though
in general Mr. Baldwin was a fundamentally lazy man,
he could meet the great occasion with an unerring eye for
the right strategy that was remarkable, for no one can examine the different stages in the delicate, even dangerous
process which resulted in the abdication of Edward VIII
without realising that every move he made was a masterly
one, for which he secured the support of the overwhelming majority of the public, and this appears the more
striking when it is remembered that the main opposition

to his policy was inspired, and, in part at least, directed, by the versatile energy of Mr. Churchill.

Mr. Bonar Law was Prime Minister for too brief a time for any real judgment to be made of how he would have used his position. Mr. Ramsay MacDonald was, obviously enough, a Prime Minister upon whom the strain of office was so great that it brought out in him some of the worst qualities in his character. He was seldom loyal for long to any of his major colleagues. He found it difficult, as in the two well-known incidents of Sir Alexander Grant's gift to him of a life-income and a car, and of the withdrawal of the Campbell prosecution, not to be evasive where he feared the result of frankness. He surrendered himself completely to the eagerly proffered embraces of "society", and, from his arrival at Ten Downing Street, he greatly preferred close private relations with his political enemies to any attempt at much more than intimacy at the official level with his friends. It is clear from the Campbell case that he was capable of grievous dishonesty; and this case was only the prelude to the supreme dishonesty of his behaviour in the crisis of 1931; and it is difficult not to believe that the rapid moral and intellectual demoralisation of his personality after that event was the outcome of inner and deep tensions he was unable to overcome. It is said that, in his two periods of office as Labour Prime Minister, he was an efficient chairman of the Cabinet. It is certainly true that, at least until 1931, while he spoke with eloquent vagueness and in large terms about the firmness with which he proposed to act, he was usually nervous to the point of vacillating timidity when it came to facing the criticisms of his policy; a good example of

I

this was his Janus-like attitude, in 1930, to the Passfield Memorandum on Palestine. In his Government of 1929, he suffered something like torture from the attacks of the Left Wing in the Labour Party; and it is not improbable that his decision in 1931 arose, if only half consciously, from a deep yearning to be free from the embarrassment of its criticism.

Mr. Neville Chamberlain was a Prime Minister of a quite different kind. He had a commonplace mind, but with the habits of regularity and order which made him an excellent chairman of a committee, even of the Cabinet, getting through business with an incisiveness and dispatch to which most of his colleagues have borne testimony. He was a man of considerable ambition, who obviously suffered a great deal from his relegation to the background by a father of overwhelming personality, and by his father's choice of his elder half-brother, Sir Austen Chamberlain, for whom his affection was deep and sincere, as the inheritor of the political mantle. Neville Chamberlain, humiliated by failure in business, and by the contempt shown him by Mr. Lloyd George in the first World War during his short tenure of high political office, drove himself into office to compensate for the injuries thus inflicted upon his self-respect. Being a deeply sensitive man, he armoured himself from attack by the swift development of an authoritarian temper and a refusal to admit to himself that there were immense limitations to the range of his mind. When he found that the road to his political promotion was swift, so that, when Mr. Baldwin became Prime Minister for the third time, he was already Chancellor of the Exchequer, with the confident know-

ledge that the succession to the leadership was his, with
the overwhelming assent of his party, he developed convictions so strong that he was really impermeable to
criticism not only from the Opposition, which he treated
with much the same contempt as that from which he had
suffered before 1922, but even from members of his own
party, whose differences with him he assumed to be the
outcome either of rival ambition or of an inability to
attain the level of his own insight. This attitude bred in
him not only a fantastic self-confidence, but a demand for
loyal obedience to his policy as the major merit in his
colleagues. He acted, virtually, as his own Foreign Secretary; and there are few things more remarkable in recent
political history than his power to bind his party to follow
him on the tragic road to "appeasement", even when it
lost him Mr. Anthony Eden and Viscount Cranborne as
colleagues, at one stage, and Sir Alfred Duff Cooper at
another. There is little to show that he was ever moved by
the opposition to his foreign policy of Mr. Churchill and
his friends. No statesman of his position was ever so easily
deceived by political gangsters like Mussolini and Hitler;
his adventure at Munich, in 1938, is at once the most
tragic and pathetic episode in misapplied self-confidence
in modern English history. He not only threw Czechoslovakia to the wolves of destruction without even the
pretence of effective consultation with its leaders about
the defence of their nation; he imposed on his Cabinet,
Sir Alfred Duff Cooper apart, the conviction that his talks
with Hitler at Munich and Godesberg had laid the foundation of permanent peace in the West, and that it was their
duty to believe this with the same simple faith by which

he was himself moved. It is, no doubt, true that two of Mr. Chamberlain's profoundest convictions were his zeal for peace and his confidence that no one would gain from a new war except Soviet Russia, which he loathed and feared. But it is nothing less than astonishing that, even with these beliefs, he should have been ready to take the word of Mussolini and Hitler that they shared his outlook. Indeed, if the *Diary* of Ciano is to be believed, whenever Mr. Eden, as Foreign Secretary, spoke sternly about Mussolini's policy to Grandi, the Italian Ambassador in London, Mr. Chamberlain, behind the back of his own colleague, sent secret messages to Grandi, for transmission to Rome, which emphasised that there was no need there to take Mr. Eden's rebukes too seriously. He lived in this amazing day-dream until, on 15th March, 1939, Hitler broke all his previous pledges by taking over the broken remains of Czechoslovakia. Then, after two days of bewildered hesitation, he broke out into a fierce denunciation of the deceptions of which he had been the willing victim, and gave guarantees of territorial integrity, which he was not in a position to implement in the absence of an understanding with Russia, to the three semi-Fascist states of Poland, Greece, and Rumania. He then, with obvious regret, began discussions with Russia for mutual understanding by methods and men whose character and status were almost an announcement in public that he was not over-anxious for agreement in Moscow, for he not only delayed negotiations until the last possible moment, but put them in charge, not of the Foreign Secretary, but of minor officials to whom full powers could not possibly have been given; and while

these were slowly winding their way to failure, he was
discussing the possibility of a settlement with Hitler by
means of dazzling financial offers of which he put one of
his Cabinet Ministers in charge. Perhaps until early
August 1939, he was living, with his colleagues, in a
twilight world which inhibited any clarity of vision.
Hitler prepared his next stroke against Poland with ease
and swiftness; and he was able to arrive at a temporary
agreement with Russia, which gave his Eastern front safeguard from attack, because Mr. Chamberlain had made it
obvious that he remained anxious to delude himself into
a renewed conviction that Hitler would become his ally
in a supreme effort for peace. Ten days after the signature
of the Russian–German Pact he was driven to the declaration of war against Germany which finally engulfed the
whole world in its flames.

I have dwelt at this length on Mr. Chamberlain's character as Prime Minister, and the policy which followed
from it, because it illustrated so supremely the dangers of
concentrating the immense powers of his office in the
hands of a second-rate man who is so wrapped up in the
truth of his own insights that he is deaf to all criticisms
of their validity. In order to impose his policy, he had to
get rid of the Permanent Secretary of the Foreign Office,
Sir Robert (now Lord) Vansittart, who was given the
kind of nominal promotion which, in fact, was intended
to relegate him to obscurity, and to replace him by Sir
Alexander Cadogan, who was lacking in the habit of
asking inconvenient questions. He sent a new Ambassador, Sir Nevile Henderson, to Berlin, who was not
only a warm friend of "appeasement", but believed that

God had chosen him to be the instrument of this high purpose. He made his chief confidant Sir Horace Wilson, a permanent civil servant, who, whatever his abilities, had neither training in, nor experience of, diplomacy. He drove out of office a Foreign Secretary and a First Lord of the Admiralty, as well as a distinguished junior Minister, because he could not bear to listen to hostile voices. He treated the opposition of the Labour Party, and of Mr. Winston Churchill and his supporters among the Tories, with something it is difficult not to describe as contempt. Yet, even when, with the outbreak of war, he saw the whole of his policy fall to pieces, he was so self-confident that, on the outbreak of war, he asked the Labour and Liberal Parties to serve under him as Prime Minister of a Coalition Government. When in the first fortnight of May 1940, he had waged war so inanely that Germany had overrun Norway, compelling the half-equipped British to withdraw, he twice repeated his offer of a Coalition under his leadership, in the conviction that, with the Low Countries invaded, and France deeply divided against itself, it was his mission to lead the European democracies to victory. He was surprised and hurt at the Labour Party's unanimous refusal to serve under him as Prime Minister; indeed, the last remark I ever heard him make was in his room at the House of Commons in mid-June, 1940, when, reflecting on the three years of his mounting failure, he said to me with obvious conviction that as he looked back on his policy, he could not see anything that, given the situation he had confronted, he would not do again. I left him wrapped up in this astonishing mood of reminiscent complacency, and

I was grateful for the thought that Mr. Winston Churchill was, despite the still obvious dissatisfaction of Mr. Chamberlain's supporters, the war-time leader of a nation at last ready to face the grim reality to meet which it had never been prepared. Nothing better illustrates the impenetrable armour of Mr. Neville Chamberlain's self-confidence than that, up to the start of the war, the only real concession he made to the passionate attacks upon his policy was to appoint Sir Thomas Inskip to the position of Minister for the Co-ordination of Defence. The choice was characteristic of the man.

I see no institutional method of altering the general character of the Prime Minister's office which would not, two exceptions apart, do more harm than good to its nature and purpose. In a general way, it is right and proper that he should receive his commission to form a Government from the King on the ground that he is the elected leader of his party; no other group can know him so intimately, and none, therefore, is better able, on the political plane, to judge why they regard him, at the time of their choice, as the representative man whom they wish to follow. Since his relationship to his colleagues is one in which, broadly speaking, his ability to trust them will be the measure of his success, his right both to choose and to dismiss them—always at his own peril—seems to me incontestable. The Australian system of choice by the party caucus evades the need to meet these matters of confidence which are often of supreme importance in the relations of a Government; and in the French system of continuous, though short-lived, Coalitions in which each group insists to the Prime Minister both upon his choice of certain men, and, hardly less, of the places they must occupy, I believe that profoundly and highly influences the tendency of a French Cabinet to move towards dissolution upon the day the Chamber has given to it its first vote of confidence. And if the Prime Minister, under our system, is really to make his leadership effective among his colleagues, the powers he has of co-ordination, of control over the Cabinet agenda, his special relation to foreign affairs and to defence, his right to decide upon the use of the patronage—though, of course, the disestablishment of the Church of England, were that to occur, would remove a heavy preoccupation from his mind— and his position as the vital intermediary between the King and the Cabinet, all seem to me necessary elements to the performance of his function. The way he handles each of them is, obviously, both a peril and a danger, alike to himself, his Government, his party, and the nation. But the answer, of course, is that he maintains himself as Prime Minister by his ability to grasp his opportunities and to avoid his dangers. He always acts in the knowledge that there is someone ready to take his place; and with powers less than these it is at least a matter of doubt whether he could maintain himself against the cabals and conspiracies which are ever being organised against him, not merely by the Tadpoles and the Tapers, to whom intrigue is the breath of life, but by the colleagues upon whom he feels most certain that he can rely. In his battle with Mr. Lloyd George at the close of 1916, Mr. Asquith had explicit assurance that he could count upon the support of Mr. Arthur Balfour; he did not know that, at the same time, Mr. Lloyd George was fully aware that he could count upon Mr. Balfour to lend him his prestige if he emerged the victor, and was able to find enough support to form a Cabinet with some prospect of stability.

I think, as I have said, that there are two exceptions to the desirability of maintaining the main contours of the Prime Minister's general authority. The first is the need to make Cabinet assent necessary before a request for a dissolution is submitted by the Prime Minister to the King. There are, of course, precedents which justify either course; and it is, no doubt, generally true that a wise Prime Minister will always consult with a few of his more important colleagues before taking so urgent a decision. But there are certain possible positions against which precautions should be taken. A Prime Minister might easily take advantage of some special wave of national emotion to profit from it; in the hysteria which briefly followed Mr. Chamberlain's claim, in 1938, that he had won "peace in our time" at Munich, it is notable that Mr. Churchill pleaded earnestly with Mr. Chamberlain not to take advantage of a situation which had still to be calmly examined. In a deeply divided Cabinet, a Prime Minister might use his personal power to ask for a dissolution in order to force his dissentient colleagues either to yield to his views or to resign from a party to which they had given a lifetime of service. Or he might use this power to arrange a Coalition behind the back of his Cabinet, or of most of its members, by a variation of the methods employed by Mr. Lloyd George to seek a Coalition in 1910, or by Mr. Ramsay MacDonald in the economic crisis of 1931. On no matter is it more important that the Prime Minister should explore the minds of his colleagues. A position like that which obtained after the devaluation of the pound in September 1949, when important Cabinet Ministers are openly asking for a dissolution, and using such newspapers as they can influence to press for it, while others speculate, and cause discussion about, possible dates, is bad for the influence of the Government in international relations, uncomfortable for trade, disturbing to the problems of party organisation, and pretty certain to take the mind of Parliament off what might be serious business, as well as to set this, and all other business, in the context of a threatened election. One sees, in the process, the friend becoming the electoral enemy. In the Parliament of 1945–50 there were few things more striking than the almost consistent support given by the Tories to Mr. Ernest Bevin against the criticisms levelled against him from the Left Wing of his own party. Yet, once the prospect of a swift dissolution began to emerge, there entered into the atmosphere of the Tory attitude, not least into that of its famous leader, a temper of dissatisfaction, even of hostility, which it is really only possible to explain as part of the preparations for an electoral campaign. In the heat and stirring of a general election, it is usually emphasised that no Minister must be spared; and the expression of dissatisfaction and anxiety for a policy which has, for the most part, been firmly supported for over four years is less honest thinking than a preparation of the base which can justify as strong an attack on Mr. Ernest Bevin as upon Mr. Aneurin Bevan or Mr. Herbert Morrison. Apart from the five years of a normal House of Commons, for which the Parliament Act makes statutory provision, a Government ought to be free, save on occasions like Munich, to choose its own time for an appeal to the electorate; but such freedom ought not to depend upon the single wish even of the first Minister of the Crown. Too much depends upon the wise discretion with which this power is used to make it dependent upon anything less than the collective responsibility of the Cabinet.

The other exception is the limits the Prime Minister may set to the circulation of Cabinet papers. The Cabinet is collectively responsible; it is still, as Bagehot said, a unit, a unit when it faces Parliament and a unit when it faces the Crown. Yet the fact remains that few Cabinets are fully informed in certain areas of vital action, especially in foreign affairs and in defence. They may be told of decisions taken only after they have gone into effect. They may be told at a moment so delayed that it is too late for them to attempt any serious discussion of the policy involved. They may be informed about one part of a policy, and not of another part which is vital to the grasp of the whole. There may be occasions when they know nothing at all of what is being done in their name, or so informed that what is told them amounts to something like deliberate falsification. In any one of these instances, of which the classical books contain many illustrations, there is no remedy for a dissident Minister except that of resignation; and he may be driven to resign, though full access to the facts might have enabled him to secure the discussion in the Cabinet out of which an honourable compromise emerges. If members of a Cabinet are to be bound by decisions taken in their names they ought to be in a position either to know and ask for the examination of those grounds, or they ought not to have been chosen as members of the Cabinet. This is a specially urgent matter where a group of Ministers takes action over the heads of other Ministers whose departmental responsibility is deeply involved. Yet it is obvious that both the Secretary of State for War and the Secretary of State for Air were unconscious instruments of three of their senior colleagues in decisions about Palestine which might well have led to war there, without even the chance of putting their views upon the decisions which had been taken. And in these instances, the situation was made worse by the fact that the Ministers who went behind the backs of the two service Ministers cannot but have realised that the action they took was bound to involve the diminution of their colleagues' authority over the officials in their own Departments.

It is clear, on any showing, that the whole *modus operandi* of the Cabinet depends upon the habits of the Prime Minister, but, even more, that little short of revolt, whether in or outside the Cabinet, can really shake his position as the master of its fortunes. It was a combination of intrigue and revolt which overthrew Mr. Asquith in 1916; it was revolt which overthrew Mr. Lloyd George in 1922; and it was revolt which overthrew Mr. Neville Chamberlain in 1940. Elections apart, a Prime Minister can virtually stay in office for as long as he chooses, provided he does not estrange a group of powerful colleagues, and is able to hold the general loyalty of the mass of his followers. Recent experience has shown that this is true whether he has a dramatic and expansive personality, like that of Mr. Churchill, or is quiet and reserved, like Mr. Attlee. The amount of reserve power that is in his hands makes it virtually impossible for any single Minister to challenge his authority; for the only way he can do so is by resignation, and that is not likely to be effective unless the swing of the wind of events is on his side. I doubt whether it can be said, all in all, that the Prime Minister's power is as great as that of the President of the United States; but in exceptional instances it may rival, if not surpass, that authority. If one considers, for example, the range of subject-matter directly under the hands of Mr. Lloyd George or of Mr. Churchill in war-time, it was hardly inferior to that of President Roosevelt; and even a strong-willed, not to say wilful, Prime Minister, like Mr. Chamberlain, had, even in peace-time, a range of authority which he directly exerted, which made him virtually Foreign Secretary and something like a Minister of Defence as well. No one, either, can seriously doubt that the Prime Minister's status has increased since the habit developed, in the first World War, of having one of his colleagues act as Leader of the House of Commons, the Prime Minister attending from time to time to answer questions, to make special announcements, and to take part in debates of exceptional importance. That has inevitably created the impression that an active participation in discussion by the Prime Minister invests the issue involved with a special character. His status, too, is enhanced by the occasional broadcasts he delivers, not so much in a political capacity as party chief, but, under the King, as the head of the nation.

There is a problem of some real significance involved

in this growth of the Prime Minister's power. It is, of course, true that great leadership carries with it great authority; but, in this case, great authority may also accrue to one, the greatness of whose leadership may fairly be regarded as doubtful. Mr. Churchill once remarked that the second World War might fitly be termed the "unnecessary war" and he took that view on the ground that, although the major and direct responsibility for it lay with Hitler, steps could have been taken in this country, at a number of points in the growth of Hitler's influence, to check it, and even to break his régime by the act of the German people themselves. It is difficult to contest this; it is obvious that the responsibility for the failure to take such steps rested mainly on the three predecessors of Mr. Churchill as Prime Minister, most of all on Mr. Chamberlain. This, clearly, gives rise to two grave questions: first, whether the Prime Minister has excessive power in proportion to that of other Cabinet Ministers, and, second, whether he has excessive power in relation to the Cabinet as a whole. Certainly, it is strange that, when Mr. Eden was Foreign Secretary, the Prime Minister felt himself entitled—if Ciano is telling the truth—to enter upon discussions with the Italian Ambassador behind the back of a colleague whose opposition to what he was doing was well known to him, was, indeed, the reason for the discussions which have been revealed; and it is hardly less strange that Mr. Eden's resignation should not have shaken a single one of his Cabinet colleagues into supporting him. Not less remarkable is the fact that Mr. Chamberlain should have gone to Munich not only without the Foreign Secretary, not only without the Permanent Head of the Foreign Office, but with Sir Horace Wilson, whose whole experience lay outside the realm of foreign affairs. Still more strange is the apparent fact that the final disposition of Czechoslovakia's fate at Munich should have been made without any reference of which we are at present aware either to the Committee of Imperial Defence or to the Chiefs of Staff Committee, when the decisions taken at Munich involved not only a heavy addition, which included the famous Skoda works, to Hitler's military strength, but also a grave alteration in the proportionate power of Nazi Germany to its main Western opponents. It is disturbing, moreover, to note that when, as a result of Munich, Sir Alfred Duff Cooper resigned, not a single other Minister followed his example. Are we to infer from this that the Cabinet has come to acquiesce in the right of the Prime Minister to play what is, in fact, an independent role over a wide range of general policy? Or is the explanation that resignation, which was once an instrument of great power, has now ceased to count? Or is the reason that, in the highest realms of policy, the Prime Minister consults so few of his colleagues that they are often confronted with what is a *fait accompli*, the background of which is so insufficiently known to them as to lessen that sense of collective responsibility which has in the past been so vital a safeguard in our system?

I do not pretend to know the answers to these questions, though I think it is right that they should be asked. It is obvious that, if we compare 1850 with 1950, or even 1900 with 1950, the centralisation of power in the Prime Minister's hands has proceeded at a swift pace, and that its judicious use is mainly dependent upon his own self-restraint; it is hardly less obvious, as the history of Mr. MacDonald and Mr. Neville Chamberlain suggests, that the absence of that self-restraint may well leave the Prime Minister in a position of commanding eminence, where there is only the chance of *ex post facto* control; and, as the events of Munich showed, that control may well come too late. This centralisation, I venture to think, is only part of a similar process that is taking place in all areas of governmental authority. At its most severe, it is shown in the passage of important local functions to the central Government, and that upon a scale which, if local government is to attract both elected and official personnel of the appropriate quality, requires a swift reorganisation both of areas and of functions. The reorganisation of local government is, however, a much easier task (though it is difficult enough) than the discovery of ways and means to the limitation of the Prime Minister's functions. I, myself, believe that the discovery is more likely to be made in the area of his relations with his party, both in and outside the House of Commons, than it is within the Cabinet itself, or in Parliament as a whole. I think it will be made in the light of a crisis or crises in which the excessive authority of the Prime Minister will be seen to have been the main source of the errors that are made. But this is purely speculative and hypothetical; and I suspect that it is wiser for me to keep to the low ground of analysis than to ascend to the mountain-top of prediction, where one is in danger of being lost in the mists that linger there.

IX

MR. AMERY'S VIEWS ON THE STRUCTURE
OF THE CABINET

Since the accession of Mr. Lloyd George to the Premiership in December 1916, there have been three experiments
in Cabinet form, and a long period, between the wars,
when it was restored to its original character. Mr. Lloyd
George made two important changes, apart from the
brief periods in which he was able to convoke a meeting
of Commonwealth Ministers with his own colleagues
to which he gave the name of the Imperial War Cabinet.
He instituted the wholly admirable and long-needed
change of providing the Cabinet with a secretariat, of
which Sir Maurice (now Lord) Hankey was the first
head, and assigning to it the functions of ensuring that the
Cabinet papers were distributed, signed for, and returned,
that proper Cabinet archives were maintained (though
the memoranda of one Cabinet cannot normally be consulted by its successor), and having the Secretary to the
Cabinet with, sometimes, an assistant secretary present,
both to draw up a minute of its proceedings, and to communicate the decisions taken to all Ministers to whose
work they were relevant. No one can doubt that this was
an important improvement on the earlier procedure when
the only record of what occurred was the normal letter
sent by the Prime Minister to the King—of which, as a
rule, the Prime Minister's private secretary kept a copy—
in which the King was informed of what had taken
place. Most of the standard biographies have some

anecdote to record of how difficult it was, after a long, and frequently rambling and confused discussion, to retain any precise recollection of what had occurred. The position is well illustrated by the note from the private secretary of Lord Hartington to the private secretary of Mr. Gladstone in 1882, when John Bright resigned over the bombardment of Alexandria. "There must have been some decision," wrote Lord Hartington's private secretary, "as Bright's resignation shows. My chief has told me to ask you what the devil *was* decided, for he be damned if he knows. Will you ask Mr. G. in more conventional and less pungent terms?" Or we have the amusing complaint of Lord Lansdowne when Queen Victoria rebuked him, during the South African War, for publishing the despatches relating to Spion Kop; those who had to give effect to Cabinet decisions, Lord Lansdowne explained, did not always carry away a clear intimation of what they were expected to do. And this uncertainty is the rule even though there were occasions when, as over the important decisions about the possible creation of peers in 1832 and 1910, a careful minute of the advice tendered to the King was compiled.

Had the Committee of Imperial Defence not existed in 1914 it is obvious that the massive work of the Cabinet could not have been attempted without some formal record; and it is possible that only Mr. Asquith's liking for the precedent of informality prevented the Cabinet Secretariat from having an earlier birth. Though there was a moment, in the brief Premiership of Mr. Bonar Law, when there was some discussion of its possible abolition, that came to nothing; and it has now become an essential part of Cabinet machinery, with a code of procedure of its own. It is now the regular practice not to circulate any draft Bills until the law officers have expressed any opinion they may have about them. Where issues concerning which the Chancellor of the Exchequer may wish to make observations are to be raised, he must be consulted in case he wishes to accompany any papers with a financial memorandum; and the Prime Minister must be satisfied that this has been done before any papers are circulated. A further rule provides that if some paper is relevant to the work of a Department the political head of which is not in the Cabinet, it may, with the consent of the Prime Minister, be circulated to the Minister in that Department for any observations he may choose to make. Normally, it is the rule that five days shall elapse between the circulation of papers and their appearance on the agenda, assuming that the Prime Minister agrees to their appearing there. This offers the other members of the Cabinet the opportunity of reading the papers, and so being in a position to discuss them; it also admits of the possibility that written comment may be circulated. The order of business on the agenda, which usually includes a statement on the international position by the Foreign Secretary, is decided by the Prime Minister. He is thus in a position to save Cabinet time by having minor matters settled between Departments, often with himself as arbitrator; and he will normally have seen to it that the Secretariat sends defence questions to the Committee on Defence, of which he is himself formally chairman, so that any long discussion of agreed committee decisions is likely to be rare. Since a standing committee of the Cabinet, the Home Affairs Committee, will normally present an agreed report on the priority of Bills, this also will tend to be a matter removed beforehand from the area of discussion and controversy. Frequently, too, individual Ministers may have discussed some matter to be raised with the Prime Minister before the Cabinet has met, and arrived with him at an agreed policy, particularly concerning defence and foreign affairs; in such cases, it is not very likely that the other members of the Cabinet will dissent from their conclusions. I remember Lord Sankey telling me that the famous Passfield White Paper on Palestine in 1930 went through the Cabinet without any discussion, since Lord Passfield had already discussed it with the Prime Minister and the Chancellor of the Exchequer, and secured their approval for it; so easily, indeed, did it go through that Lord Passfield was overwhelmed with surprise when its publication raised a storm of anger among Zionists all over the world. Lord Sankey himself told me that, knowing of this pre-Cabinet agreement, and being heavily burdened at the time, he had not himself read the Passfield paper when it was originally before the Cabinet, and only did so when the matter came up for reconsideration. Here, as in the well-known dispute between Lord Birkenhead and Lord Curzon, the proof the secretariat can produce that the Minister has signed for the receipt of a particular document is no sort of guarantee that he will have read it by the time that its fate is being decided.

Though there are limits to the usefulness of the Secretariat and, as was shown in the period when Mr.

Lloyd George used to by-pass Lord Curzon as Foreign Secretary, the possible danger that, under a Prime Minister of large ambitions, it may become an instrument for making policy rather than of simply recording that it has been made, it has proved an invaluable innovation. There is, I think, far graver doubt about Mr. Lloyd George's second invention, that of the War Cabinet with a small number of members, at the outset five, to whom, from 1917–18, Field-Marshal Smuts was added, even though he was not a member of either House of Parliament. Of these six, only Mr. Bonar Law, as Chancellor of the Exchequer, held an actual administrative post; the rest, to quote Mr. Amery's phrase, were "entirely free from all Departmental responsibilities, and in a position to give their whole time to the thinking out, shaping and execution of policy". Both Mr. Amery himself, who was, from 1916 to 1919, one of the two political assistant secretaries to the War Cabinet, and Mr. Lloyd George have indicated their strong preference for the small Cabinet of Ministers with no heavy Departmental burdens, over the normal Cabinet with a membership of between eighteen and twenty-two or twenty-three, or Mr. Churchill's war-time Cabinet, most of the members of which took charge of a great Department. Mr. Amery, in a skilful defence of his choice, notes the advantage of the freedom from the heavy burden of responsibility for administration, the value of being able to summon Departmental Ministers and their advisers only when they were relevant to the business of the day, the value of having Ministerial Committees presided over by a Minister of high authority, free from immersion in Departmental detail, able, for this reason, to dominate the Ministerial Committees and to get Cabinet support for their conclusions. Mr. Lloyd George, in his *War Memoirs*, is even more enthusiastic about the working of the experiment he initiated, though his argument for it lacks, I think, the brilliant selectivity of the case as presented by Mr. Amery.

I am persuaded, despite Mr. Amery's great authority, to believe that he has overstated his case. There were difficulties in the working of Mr. Lloyd George's Cabinet to which either he gives little attention, or no attention at all. It is, of course, true that all decisions were in the hands, first of five, and later of six, superior Ministers, who could use the Cabinet Secretariat to see that these were made fully known to the Departments. It is also true that the War Cabinet could discuss the large outlines of policy with an intimacy possible in a small committee, but rarely achieved in a Cabinet with some twenty Ministers most of whom have to bear administrative burdens as well. But that is really not the whole story. Mr. Balfour, as Foreign Secretary, attended practically every meeting of the War Cabinet. Nearly every question of serious importance involved the attendance of several Ministers who would bring their chief officials with them for support; and it was not an infrequent occurrence for anything up to twenty-five people to be in the Cabinet room at the same time, some of them Ministers who did not feel that their case was getting adequate attention, others officials who were never quite certain whether their role was merely to support their political chiefs, or to offer, if asked, their personal views with the risk that involved to the ease of their relations with their Ministers when they returned to their Departmental duties. There were Ministers who did not lightly accept the authority of the War Cabinet chairman of a Ministerial Committee, and would put up a stiff fight against decisions they did not like, either with the War Cabinet itself, or in secret conclave with the Prime Minister. The system not only tended to depress the authority of the Departmental Minister with his officials, since some of these could find their way round him, by devious routes, to Mr. Lloyd George. There was also a kind of Ministerial hierarchy which gave birth to a good deal of quarrelling and jealousy. There were Ministers who could see Mr. Lloyd George every day whenever they wished, either by reason of party status, or because, like Sir Eric Geddes, they were his personal favourites; there were Ministers who, with some effort, could usually get private access to him, as a rule to secure his support for a policy to which closely interested colleagues were opposed; and there were Ministers never important enough to see him at all. Mr. Lloyd George himself, moreover, has made plain to us that he had to cope with intrigues between his Departmental Ministers of importance in their parties over issues in which they disliked a War Cabinet decision; we know enough of the relations between Lord Derby, Sir William Robertson, and General Haig to know that they made Mr. Lloyd George approach all problems in which the two soldiers were concerned with a hesitation not normally characteristic of his habits as Prime Minister. Mr. Amery says nothing of the amazing intrigues, both for and against the policies of the War Cabinet, in which

Sir Henry Wilson engaged both as C.I.G.S. and as the British representative on the Supreme Allied War Council, of which it is impossible to believe that the War Cabinet was not aware. He does not discuss the decisions Mr. Lloyd George made without even the pretence of consultation with his colleagues. Nor, very notably, does he analyse the important speech of Lord Curzon in the House of Lords in which he explained the confusion and Departmental warfare to which the War Cabinet system gave rise. It is, perhaps, a minor matter that, after the War, Lord Milner would accept no promises from Mr. Lloyd George that were not in writing; and that Mr. Amery fails to remember that a good deal of the unity in the War Cabinet arose not out of either its freedom from responsibility for Departmental work, or from its reduction in size, but rather from the fact that, Field-Marshal Smuts apart, its members had to keep together lest any signs of disagreement should offer to Mr. Asquith, as leader of the Opposition, the chance to overthrow them. The War Cabinet of 1916 succeeded partly because of the loyalty of Mr. Bonar Law to Mr. Lloyd George, and partly because, since Mr. Lloyd George had really no party considerations to take seriously into account as in the Coalition of 1915, there was no difference of view between its various members.

I wholly agree with Mr. Amery that the traditional Cabinet of twenty members, or thereabouts, is no longer a satisfactory instrument. It is too large for intimacy, and there is no doubt that, because of its size, its vital work is prepared by the Prime Minister and a few principal colleagues, who then ask for an approval from the remainder which it is nearly impossible for them to with-hold. It is also clear that, as one goes outside a group of at most a dozen Ministers, one arrives at men whose opinion is not likely to weigh very much, who rarely concern themselves with any of the large general problems the Cabinet must decide, and are in the Cabinet less be-cause of an anxiety to use their counsel than because it has been traditional for their offices to carry with them membership of the Cabinet. Mr. Attlee, following up the device upon which Mr. Churchill placed so much reliance during the second World War, has given the Ministers of a number of Departments, like National Insurance, Fuel and Power, Supply, Food, and the three Service Departments, the status of Cabinet Ministers while excluding them from its actual membership. But this is really not very satisfactory. They attend when their special problems are under consideration, but, like their analogues in the period of the Lloyd George War Cabinet, they are not in the Cabinet for matters outside their Department's concern. Yet it is reasonable to guess that the Minister of National Insurance, Mr. James Griffiths, and the Secretary of State for War, Mr. Shin-well, have far higher party standing, and are likely to be more influential with the Prime Minister, than the Secretary of State for Scotland, Mr. Arthur Woodburn, or the Secretary of State for Commonwealth Relations, Mr. Philip Noel-Baker, who are in the Cabinet, with the right to speak on all questions and, should the very rare occasion arise when a vote is taken, cast their vote upon an issue which some of their colleagues outside the Cabinet have no necessary right to know of, much less to discuss. Both the Scottish Office and the Department of Commonwealth Relations are in the Cabinet less because of the inherent importance of their functions than because the exclusion from it of the Ministers in charge of them would cause anger and resentment in Scotland, and in the Dominions, by the blow to the prestige of their status it would involve. In the same way, were any Prime Minister to satisfy the Welsh ambition to have a separate Secretary for Wales, he would have to put the new Minister in the Cabinet itself lest exclusion from it injure the pride of Welshmen.

Nor do I dissent from Mr. Amery's careful argument against the form that Mr. Churchill gave to his Cabinet from 1940 to the break-up of the war-time Coalition with the withdrawal of the Labour Party from it shortly after V.E. Day. Apart from Mr. Churchill himself, who was both Prime Minister and Minister of Defence, and Mr. Attlee, who as Deputy Prime Minister held several posts in succession of which only one, the old Dominions Office, involved any serious volume of Departmental duties, Mr. Churchill invited into his Cabinet Mr. Bevin as Minister of Labour, Mr. Arthur Greenwood (whom he retired fairly early) as Minister without Portfolio, Mr. Morrison as Minister of Home Security and Home Secretary, Mr. Eden as Foreign Secretary, Lord Leathers as Minister of War Transport, Lord Beaverbrook, at the first stage as Minister of Aircraft Production, in a second and brief incarnation as Minister of Production, and, in a final character, as Lord Privy Seal. He invited Sir John Anderson to sit in the War Cabinet, after a period outside it as Home Secretary, first as Lord President, and later as Chancellor of the Exchequer. On Sir Stafford Cripps' return from Russia in 1941, Mr. Churchill made him Leader of the House of Commons, with a place in the War Cabinet, but, later, made him Minister of Aircraft Production, without a seat in the War Cabinet. This body itself had eight members; though, as Mr. Amery has pointed out, there were, outside it, in May 1945, forty-one Ministers of Cabinet rank, among them the Minister of Information who, though he was not a member of the War Cabinet, invariably attended its meetings. Lord Halifax, moreover, though he was persuaded by Mr. Churchill to go to Washington as Ambassador, nevertheless ranked as a member of the War Cabinet in the periods when he was home on leave, and wished to attend its meetings. It is quite obvious that there was no logical structure in Mr. Churchill's methods, but that it represented, in part, his recognition of the status of some colleagues in their respective parties, and also his personal preferences for others of his colleagues. He sought also to persuade Mr. Lloyd George to join his inner circle as a Minister without Portfolio; and though Mr. Lloyd George refused, mainly on grounds of age, it is said that Mr. Churchill consulted him with some frequency, in the light of Mr. Lloyd George's exceptional knowledge in handling a global war. The only principle, this is to say, that underlay the War Cabinet that Mr. Churchill built was that he found it most to his liking in the form he gave to it. In the special circumstances he confronted, and the exceptional functions he undertook as Prime Minister, that is probably as good a principle as any other he could have chosen.

But Mr. Churchill's formula was an individual one; and I think most observers would agree that it was unsuitable as a model for times of peace. It seems to me not less obvious that the traditional Cabinet, of which that of Mr. Attlee is only a variation, is equally unsuited to the times in which we live. First of all, it contains a number of members whose Departmental work is so heavy that they only stray from its demands into the field of general policy when there comes up some issue so vital that it drives their normal preoccupation with their own daily work into the background. Secondly, it contains a number of Ministers whose serious intrusion, with any persistence, into the general field of policy-making, above all in international affairs, would very probably be resented and lead to their receiving a word of advice from the Prime Minister upon the wisdom of being seen, and not heard. Thirdly, moreover, there is an area of policy, of which the handling of atomic energy is the outstanding example, which, in any effective way, does not come before the Cabinet at all, though its members are, of course, collectively responsible for the outcome. A great deal, fourthly, of the Cabinet's work is now done through committees, many of which contain not only Ministers, or their Parliamentary under-secretaries, but high permanent officials, whether on the Service side, like the Chiefs of Staff, or on the civilian side, which, when the outcome of their deliberations is strongly supported by the Prime Minister, practically make the approval or disapproval of the Cabinet as a whole, very much a matter of routine; indeed an attempt to discuss a committee's report at any length would probably arouse a good deal of resentment. But, even with the growth of the Committee System within the Cabinet, it may be taken for granted that the serious discussion of future policy, as distinct from immediate routine business, rarely comes before the Cabinet until the Prime Minister, and a small number of colleagues whom he has chosen, have discussed it together informally. And where a Labour Government, like Mr. Attlee's, is in office, the making of policy for the next general election is, in the first instance, a matter for the National Executive Committee of the Labour Party. That Committee will be careful to consult with all Ministers about any proposals it may be considering which fall within their jurisdiction, and, in most instances, give serious weight to their views; but its responsibility will be to the delegates at the Conference which considers its programme, and not to the Cabinet as a whole, or even to the Prime Minister, great as will be the authority it is certain to attach to his opinion.

When, therefore, Mr. Amery suggests that the traditional Cabinet should be replaced by a small Cabinet, on the model of Mr. Lloyd George's War Cabinet, in which the members have no Departmental responsibility, and are thus set free to consider long-term policy as distinct from the routine of day-to-day administration, the answer to his point is that even if this fitted the character of the Conservative Party, all the organs of which are merely advisory to its leader, they are wholly unsuited to the character of the Labour Party which, in the making of long-term policy, gives great respect to the leader of the Parliamentary Labour Party, who is Prime Minister

by reason of being so chosen, but would not permit itself
to be dominated by him. In any case, moreover, I do
not find it easy to believe that the separation of policy and
administration could be accomplished with the ease Mr.
Amery seems to imagine, by setting up, under the official
chairmanship of the Prime Minister, and on the model of
the Defence Committee, what Mr. Amery terms "a
group of standing committees for the study of policy in
the main fields of External Affairs, Economics, and Social
Welfare, each with its own adequate research and planning staff". As Mr. Amery conceives them, "these staffs
should not be self-contained bodies, but, like the joint
Intelligence and Planning Staffs developed in the last
war, should be manned by members of the intelligence and
planning staffs of their several offices at what is known in
government circles as 'the official level' ". Mr. Amery
thus depicts for us a non-departmental Cabinet of half
a dozen members, which, on one side, deals with the
daily work of the Departments, and settles their problems
after consultation with the Ministers concerned. On the
other side, this Cabinet will have "regular meetings
definitely set aside for the discussion of future policy".
In its first capacity, Mr. Amery proposes to set up *ad hoc*
committees, each provided with a chairman from the
Cabinet who will guide its deliberations and steer it to its
conclusions. But the "policy-making" standing committees of the Cabinet, with the Prime Minister as their
chairman, will each have a standing Deputy Chairman,
chosen by him from amongst his direct colleagues, who
would control and organise the work of the research and
planning staffs; and each such Deputy Chairman would

be what Mr. Amery terms "the recognised Policy Minister for his group of departments", at once in touch, in one capacity, with their day-to-day business, and able, in the other, so to relate research and planning to the work of his group that he can advise the Cabinet about the direction future policy should take. Mr. Amery also approves the suggestion of Lord Sankey that in defence matters, and with issues which stand somewhat apart from the normal conflict of parties, the Leaders of the Opposition might be regularly associated with the work of the Standing Committees which, on his plan, would deal with long-term preparations for the future.

I do not for one moment deny the persuasiveness of Mr. Amery's scheme, though I suspect that he sees it in operation through an excessively roseate view of what happened in Mr. Lloyd George's War Cabinet of 1916–19. I think, too, that he omits to note that much of what was best in the operation of that Cabinet was due to the fact that it was worked under the immediate imperatives of war, which always gives exceptional authority to the Prime Minister and his intimate group of advisers, just as it permits him to go far beyond the ranks of professional politicians in his choice of Ministers. Great as is the authority of the Prime Minister, it lacks that halo of exceptionality in peace-time; and the range of the men from whom he can choose his Ministers is necessarily abridged by the claims of the party system. This is a minor point. What I find a central weakness in Mr. Amery's proposals has two sides. The first is his failure to realise the fundamental importance of a maxim laid down by Sir Henry Taylor, whose remarkable treatise, *The Statesman*, Mr. Amery himself aptly quotes with generous admiration. "He who has in his hands the execution of measures", wrote Sir Henry, "is in very truth the master of them." Mr. Churchill was the master of war strategy in Britain from 1940 until 1945 because he was himself the Minister of Defence, and, therefore, not only in control of the Defence Committee, even when he acted through the medium of Lord Ismay, but in control, also, of the Chiefs of Staffs Committee, which enabled him directly to unify the strategy of three forces; and the directives he prints in the remarkable appendix to the second volume of his account of the war of 1939 make plain how deeply his fingers went into every aspect not only of conceiving policy, but also of watching it through to the final stage of execution.

I venture to doubt whether a "recognised Policy Minister" could seriously hope to control with any such fullness a group of Departments the Ministers in control of which would each have a mastery of the details of their daily work to a knowledge of which he could not pretend in anything like the same degree. Nor do I believe that Mr. Amery is right in concluding that, on the planning, as distinct from the current affairs, side of his proposed system the strain "on the departmental loyalty" of the civil servants "as a result of their dual capacity" would be as easily overcome as he imagines. Everything would, I think, depend upon the respective personalities of the "recognised Policy Minister", on the one hand, and the Departmental Minister, on the other. The relations between the "Policy Minister" and the Departmental Minister, and the ease they would feel in their relations to Mr. Amery's conceptions of the Cabinet, would, I suggest, be very different if the first were, say, Lord Beaverbrook, and the second, Mr. Ernest Bevin, than if they were respectively, Mr. Eden and Mr. Bevin; and what would be true of the Ministers would be true, also, of their officials. Sir Alexander Cadogan must have played a very different role as Permanent Secretary of the Foreign Office from the role of his predecessor, Lord Vansittart. Sir Horace Wilson's relation to Mr. Neville Chamberlain as Prime Minister must have raised many problems for both the Permanent Secretary to the Treasury and the Secretary to the Cabinet, different from any they confronted before that fateful partnership was formed. Mr. Amery points to the Planning Staff appointed by Sir Stafford Cripps in March 1947 as what he wants, though lacking "the ministerial co-ordination" he regards as essential. But it is, of course, obvious that the Planning Staff set up by Sir Stafford Cripps was given the shape he gave it precisely because he wanted to be its master. Once the element of "ministerial co-ordination" entered it, Sir Stafford Cripps' authority over the Joint Planning Staff would have been far less easy to operate with any smoothness. Though I have deep respect for Mr. Amery's experience and judgment, I am convinced that co-ordination, whether ministerial or Departmental, is far more difficult to achieve than he imagines, especially when Departmental traditions are deep-rooted, and the personalities concerned are men of character who hold strongly to a view that they have put forward with vigour. It is, for example, revealed by Mr. Churchill himself, that, even when he was Prime Minister, his own

L

strongly expressed wishes were not able to overcome the eager desire of the War and Foreign Offices to prevent the formation of a Jewish division in the Middle East; and the two Departments had their way even though the Jews were rendering important services to Great Britain, while the Arab states were pro-Nazi, and the Arabs in Palestine mostly stood by as sullen spectators of one of the great crises in our history. If in the face of a completely outmoded tradition in the two Departments of friend-ship for the Arabs—a tradition the folly of which was demonstrated beyond doubt when the British Mandate for Palestine was surrendered—Mr. Churchill felt it impossible to override the tradition, there are few other Ministers who would have had the courage and tenacity to do so.

I wholly agree, if I may say so, with Mr. Amery's insistence upon the importance of having Cabinet meet-ings which deal, not with the current day's business, but with long-term policy. But I suggest that it is largely unrealistic to think of holding such Cabinet meetings in the absence of the Departmental Ministers who will be concerned in implementing the policy agreed upon. For every discussion of general principles of a long-term character is bound to raise a hundred questions of detail upon which the advice of the Departmental Minister, if he has any merit at all, will be of decisive importance; and there is a whole range of issues decision upon which cannot wisely be left to the Cabinet if the lines it is to follow are to be certain of commanding the support of party opinion, on the one hand, and of the general body of unattached voters upon the other. The issue of a

Second Chamber is a good example of this type. With the passage of the Parliament Act of 1949, there is pretty general agreement that a thoroughgoing reconstruction of the composition of the House of Lords is urgent. Mr. Amery, surely, would not argue that his half-dozen Cabinet Ministers could arrive at a conclusion on these matters without extensive consultation reaching far beyond themselves. A Labour Cabinet would certainly have to consult the Parliamentary Labour Party, the National Executive and the Annual Conference of the Party, as well as to arrive, if it could, at agreement with the Opposition, on the character of a new Second Chamber; and, if it could not reach that agreement, the scheme behind which it decided to stand would have to win support from the rank and file of its supporters, as well as from the unattached voters, by a carefully organised campaign of conferences and meetings before it would be safe to assume that it would be wise to go forward with it. If the Tory Party, moreover, stood firmly by their views that there must not only be an element in the new Second Chamber chosen by the present hereditary peers themselves, but also that the Speaker's right to define a Money Bill solely in the light of his own judgment be transferred to a joint committee of both Houses under his chairmanship, I can conceive no Cabinet, whatever its nature, which rested upon the support of the Labour Party, which would venture finally to decide either of these issues without a great deal of preliminary public consultation. I hardly need to remind you that though Mr. Attlee's Cabinet was agreed upon the need for maintaining a system of national training for defence

purposes, it was careful to discuss this principle with all
the major consultative organs of the Labour Movement
before it finally resolved to put the system into operation.

It may be said by those who think like Mr. Amery that
this is not the kind of issue in future policy-making which
any Cabinet such as he contemplates would discuss and
settle without arrangements for widespread external
consultation. Let me, then, take two further examples.
When Mr. Attlee, early in 1947, took his great and brave
decision about the future relations between Great Britain
and India, he and his colleagues not only had behind them
a generation of strong support from successive Annual
Conferences of the Labour Party—including one, as
recent as 1944, in which the delegates insisted on going
much further than the National Executive Committee
was ready to do—but he brought it into being amidst
what it is hard to refrain from terming something like a
world debate. He had to explain the recall of Lord
Wavell, and his replacement by Lord Mountbatten as
Viceroy. He had to explain the function of the special
mission, headed by Sir Stafford Cripps—whose effort
had failed in 1942—which went out for the purpose of
conducting direct negotiations on the spot. When agreement with India and Pakistan was reached, he had to get
the assent of the other Dominions to the new status they
thus assumed. All this had then to secure Parliamentary
approval after debate; and when India, in 1949, decided
upon becoming an independent republic associated with
the British Commonwealth of Nations, recognising the
special position of the King as its head, Parliamentary
sanction was again necessary for giving formal legality

to the new arrangements. I can well understand that the first stage in the making of Mr. Attlee's Indian policy could have taken the form of the kind of Cabinet discussion Mr. Amery has in mind. But I am bound to point out, first, that, in some shape, it would have done so under almost any system, and, second, that what gave the policy its validity was the background in which it was set, and the authority it secured by the confirmation of public discussion.

Let me take a final example of decisive importance. It is well known that our policy in relation to atomic energy is largely kept in the Prime Minister's own hands, with counsel from a small body of chosen colleagues, in the light of advice offered by scientific and defence experts. One of the aspects of that policy has been the decision firmly to support the Acheson-Lilienthal Plan for the control of Atomic Energy which was placed before the United Nations by Mr. Baruch on behalf of the United States. It was, of course, rejected by Soviet Russia, and now that Soviet Russia has itself been able to make and explode an atomic bomb—perhaps more than one—it is clear that a scheme of control built upon the assumption that the American Government possessed a monopoly of the "know-how" so essential to the engineering, as distinct from the purely physical side, of the bomb's manufacture, is not only obsolete, but a source of international irritation when it is pressed for acceptance by the United Nations in circumstances so different from those of its original formulation. Wisdom now clearly indicates that the present deadlock at Lake Success, which threatens the danger of a race for supremacy in atomic weapons, should be broken with the least possible delay. If, as I should hope, the British Government were to take the initiative in attempting to break the deadlock by working out, and putting forward, a new and more acceptable scheme adapted to the changed circumstances, no one, I take it, assumes for one moment that a matter of such moment would be an ordinary item in the agenda of a Cabinet usually concerned with making up its mind about current affairs. The Prime Minister would obviously want it to be examined by a special group of his colleagues, to whose opinions he attached exceptional weight, and from whom he would exact the time and thought necessary to read all the papers the experts would put in, to hear the physicist and the soldier, the airman and the engineer, the chemist and the admiral, put their views, and be able to cross-examine them about their implications so as to arrive at a body of proposals which could be submitted with some prospect of their acceptance at Lake Success. But I cannot myself see that the chance of arriving at such a body of proposals is greatly increased by the separation of Ministers who make policy from Ministers who are concerned with the details of administration in a special Department of the Government. For, first of all, it is a question of the men available. Any first-rate Minister knows how to dispose of his time so that he is not bogged down in the details of his Department; perhaps the most important part of his job as a Minister is the separation of the essential from the inessential, and the power to judge the capacity of his chief officials to keep themselves sufficiently free from immersion in detail so that they can always find time to look afresh at the basic principles of their policy. And, in any case, it is of the essence of what Mr. Amery calls "current administration" that its problems are looked at in the light of policy so that they can be fitted into the categories which permit of national solution. Anyone who ran the War Office, for example, with the insight and imagination that Lord Haldane brought there in the critical years from 1905 to 1911 gets exactly the kind of training in policy-making by building a direct relation between the act and the idea which Mr. Amery seems to want in the special kind of "thinking" Cabinet he proposes. If I may use an analogy upon a much humbler level, I think the evidence is convincing that the university teacher is at his best when he combines teaching with research. It is important for him to live in an atmosphere where it is his task not merely to enlarge the boundaries of knowledge in his subject, but to clarify for his students the significance of the new frontiers and to attempt to prove that his choice of route to them has been intelligent and wise. An obvious illustration of this theme is the illustrious tradition of the Cavendish Laboratory at Cambridge where, from the time of Clerk Maxwell until to-day, its director and his colleagues have, by the combination of their own researches with the supervision of their students' first experiences in what is meant by the discovery of new knowledge, been able to make their remarkable institution a great mountain-peak in the range of those laboratories which attempt fundamental research. That Lord Rutherford would have been a great physicist even if he had confined himself to research alone, I am not, of course, concerned to deny. But that he speeded up the whole process of vital discovery by the daily exchange of ideas with the younger men who came to him for the chance of being inspired by the range and depth of his ideas is, I think, shown conclusively by the work done in the Cavendish while he was its Director. He proved remarkably, what is also true in politics, that the man who can carry his own heavy load of work with care, is by far the most likely to find time and thought to ease the path for those who bear a heavy load also in an area related to his field.

I suspect, therefore, that what is really important in Mr. Amery's scheme for a Cabinet is not its separation between those who make policy and those who give it Departmental application, but his eloquent and vigorous insistence that, however the Cabinet be constructed, it must distinguish between policies of long range, built upon research and thought which may occupy long periods of effort, and policies which have to be settled at once in order to enable swift action to be taken upon them; of the latter type, for example, a Cabinet called to decide whether the Emergency Powers Act should be invoked when there is a sudden and widespread strike in a vital industry is a sufficient illustration. I am sure, further, that Mr. Amery is wholly right in rejecting the proposal, strongly urged, a generation ago, by the Haldane Committee on the Machinery of Government, of a special Ministry of Research, whose inquiries would be divorced from the responsibilities of actual administration. The proposal was a mistaken one for the same reason that Lord Beveridge's enthusiastic support for an Economic General Staff was, as I have sought to show elsewhere,[1] a mistaken enthusiasm. In a broad way, research that is to affect policy must be controlled by those who are directing policy that they hope to implement in the fairly foreseeable future; and, if some of it requires specialists, they must be in the closest possible touch with the civil servants who are actually engaged in administration to which that research is related. Neither at the Ministerial nor at the official level is research likely to be directly relevant to planning for action if it is kept apart from the sense of reality which comes from an effective relation with those whose business it will be to translate its results into policy and action. A Ministry of Research would never disentangle itself from conflict with Ministries the Intelligence Departments of which are not concerned to see things *sub specie aeternitatis*. The researchers must be in as direct a contact with the administrators as were the participants in operational research in contact with the High Command in the field during the second World War. It is this contact, also, which is missing in the idea of an Economic General Staff which, originally proposed by Sir Hubert Henderson, has been publicised with such ardour by Lord Beveridge. The Economic General Staff would be in great danger of rapidly becoming a series of miniature Royal Commissions, in large part dependent upon the relevant Departments for their material, and brooding upon its possible meanings within a framework of ideas either determined within its own hierarchy, and not, therefore, necessarily helpful to the Department concerned, since the responsibility for the Department's framework of ideas is necessarily that of

[1] cf. *Parliamentary Government in England*, pp. 267 et seq.

its Minister; or it might become a pool of economists and statisticians from which additional aid could be given to the Intelligence Branch of a Department concerned to work out the basis of legislative or administrative action more quickly than its normal complement would be able to do. Obviously, in the second case, it ceases to be an Economic General Staff; and the whole value of the specialised techniques which its members possess will depend upon the depth of their immersion in the special problems of the Department to which they are sent. It is here worth while noting that a large part of the value of Lord Beveridge's Report on social insurance came from the fact that, as an official of the Ministry of Labour, he had been closely involved in its day-to-day problems for many years, and that, even after he left the Ministry, those problems remained among his major preoccupations. And if we take Mr. N. Kaldor's remarkable appendix to Lord Beveridge's *Full Employment in a Free Society*, it is clear that much of its value depends upon the fact that he was given the framework of assumptions within which he made his brilliant calculations.

This kind of research belongs to a different order of thought from that which occupies the attention of the Medical Research Council, the Department of Scientific and Industrial Research, the Central Statistical Office, and similar bodies. They are, quite properly, detached from policy-making, in the important sense that they have no direct responsibility for what is done with the results of their inquiries. A significant table compiled by the Central Statistical Office may lead the Chancellor of the Exchequer or, it may be, the President of the Board of Trade, to lay some proposals before the Cabinet. The Medical Research Council may assist a physiological investigation which may result in the Minister of Health making new proposals to the Cabinet, or issuing a new circular to the local authorities. It is, of course, true that most of these research bodies are directly under the jurisdiction of the Lord President of the Council, and that he must deal with questions about them in the House of Commons. But he is more concerned with them in the way in which the Chancellor of the Exchequer is concerned with the University Grants Committee than with the way in which the Minister of Health is concerned with the medical men in his Department. On the expert advice of a number of committees, the Lord President, after agreement with the Chancellor of the Exchequer, provides so many millions for research into projects which, despite their often supreme importance, have only a remote and indirect bearing on the making of political policy. It is conceivable that a grant from the Medical Research Council for further investigation into the properties of a half-known drug which may be useful in the cure of the common cold would become a subject for a question in the House of Commons; and it is possible that, on the estimates for the Lord President's office, he might be challenged to show that he is spending enough money, and enough money wisely, on matters like cancer research, or the investigation of treatment for silicosis, or for the work of the National Physical Laboratory. But in no instances of this character is there any supposition that policy-making by the Government is immediately involved. If the Medical Research Committee decided to advise the Lord President that more money should be spent on the endowment of vitamin research, that would be as unpolitical in its nature as if a university were to persuade the University Grants Committee to provide a larger sum to enable it to use more time to be spent by its specialists in politics and history in preparing for publication the rich treasure of Burke's *Letters* which Lord Fitzwilliam has deposited in the public reference library of the city of Sheffield.

Research, that is to say, which is intended to lead to political action in the reasonably foreseeable future must be carried out in conjunction with both Ministers and officials who are likely to be concerned with that political action. On this aspect of government structure, there is, I believe, no real answer to the way in which Mr. Amery approaches the problem. That makes it more difficult for me to understand why, when this principle is so clear to him, he should in reality abandon it at the level of Ministerial relations. For the fact is that his Cabinet of non-departmental Ministers, each of whom takes charge of a group of subjects, and controls long-term policy-making about them, is faced by two difficulties as real as any confronted by the present Cabinet system. Most of the Cabinet Minister's time will be occupied by the daily supervision of the Departments of which he is in charge; and any failure to get on amicably with the political heads of those Departments will necessarily invade the time at the disposal of the Cabinet, as Mr. Amery conceives it, for the long-range making of policy. The abler the Departmental Minister is, moreover, the more difficult will the Cabinet Minister find it to control him where they disagree. Not only will he strain the loyalty of the officials in the Department; he will need to have an acquaintance with its papers at least equal to that of the Departmental Minister concerned, if he is to meet him on equal terms. If to this there is added not only the time the Cabinet Minister must spend in the direction of planning in the area allotted to him by reason of the Departments over which he has control, but the time he must spend, in the Cabinet itself, helping to resolve differences in other areas between other Cabinet Ministers and their Departmental teams, it is at least not obvious that the freedom from immersion in current affairs, of which Mr. Amery speaks with so much emphasis, is likely to be outstanding in volume. When to this there is further added the time he is bound to devote to Parliament, on the one hand, and to necessary public engagements on the other, it does not seem unfair to conclude that, on Mr. Amery's new model, the new type of Cabinet Minister he envisages is likely to carry at least as heavy a burden as the old type. The only exception I can see to this probability is when he is fortunate enough to preside over a group of Departmental Ministers who take his word as law. On experience, he will only encounter this good fortune when his political subordinates are devoid of ambition, and regard themselves as men of the second or third rank whose hopes of promotion are measured, in their own esteem, as thin and weak. Upon this, it is sufficient to say that there are rarely more than half a dozen Ministers in any Cabinet who do not sometimes reflect upon the possibility that a change in political relations within their party may not result in their advancement to a higher, and, sometimes, the highest, place. It is well worth while to reflect upon the speed with which Mr. Neville Chamberlain transformed himself from a local councillor, full of doubts rooted in his eclipse by other members of his family, to a self-assured Chancellor of the Exchequer, convinced that his Prime Minister was lingering too long upon the stage.

If we agree with a long line of distinguished observers, going back to somewhere about the time of that great administrator, Sir Robert Peel, and unlikely to end with that skilful power to summarise his wide experience that Mr. Amery displays, that a Cabinet varying in size from eighteen to twenty-four is too big, with what other possibilities are we left? There is Mr. Amery's own scheme, previously expounded, built on first-hand knowledge, and at least squarely confronting the difficulties involved. Yet, for the reasons I have already given, Mr. Amery's scheme does not seem to me as simple and straightforward as he seems to think. I do not deny its attractions, but I think it would require supermen to make it work with any smoothness, and the superman in politics is far more rare than we like to think. We have plenty of able men, sound, hard-working, devoted, even generous and selfless. But I am far less sure than Mr. Amery that the delicate equilibrium of the relations he imagines has much chance of remaining stable for any length of time; certainly there was little of that stability in the War Cabinet of Mr. Lloyd George, which he offers us as a model; still less, I fear, in the War Cabinet of Mr. Churchill, the structure of which he did not approve. I am tempted, indeed, to suggest that the generalisation upon which all Mr. Amery's model is based, namely that you can separate policy from administration, is based upon the same fallacy as that which separates theory from practice, "fundamental" research in science from "applied" research. The truth is that each of these categories is not something inherent in a reality outside ourselves, but an emphasis in our own minds upon the way in which we approach a problem. The real weakness of the political mind is its impatience with fundamental thinking as the basis for the action towards which it is led. In the result, it places excessive reliance upon the experts who serve it in different fields, and assumes that, since they have already done the fundamental thinking in their own specialism, the politicians are free to give practical form to theoretical conclusions, and that they can do it the more effectively because they are men of the world, with all the wisdom and common sense that comes from experience therein.

I am sure that this is a wholly mistaken approach. Wherever there is a place for the specialist, it is not at the point where the Cabinet Minister translates his principles into policy or administration. The expert's findings must be combined with an imaginative insight into men and women whose outlook is at once more traditional and more experimental than is often realised by the politician, if a successful policy is to emerge; and no administrator will ever apply policy creatively unless he is profoundly aware of the philosophy which underlies and drives along the decisions it is his business to impose. That is why it is so urgent not to separate, as Mr. Amery does, the Minister who looks to the future from the Minister who is concerned with the present. For the man who decides upon current affairs is, in fact, the man who shapes the future. He gives its form to the matrix upon which new ideas are to be stamped—and if he fails to prepare the form of matrix that is required, the new idea will be stamped upon it only with difficulty, and may fail to get stamped upon it at all. That, in fact, was why Sir Henry Taylor said, in the phrase I have already quoted, that "he who has in his hands the execution of measures, is in truth the very master of them". The Prime Minister always apart, Mr. Amery's idea of a Cabinet as a collection of Ministers thinking firmly and imaginatively about the future, with a day or two off each week in which they consider the flow of current affairs, or, maybe, the cross-currents in the stream that prevent the boat from going forward, is exactly that divorce of theory from practice that is as fatal not only to getting things done as they should be done, but getting them so done that what is achieved is itself a preparation for the next achievement. I am not arguing that a Minister who reflects upon the future must bury himself in his Departmental papers; but I do not think that the best way to prevent that burial is mainly to make of him a brooding omnipresence in the sky who darts, two or three times a week, down to earth, and then flies back to whatever special area of the stars the Prime Minister may have allocated to him as his special residence.

I am arguing the quite explicit thesis that a good Cabinet Minister is a man who is always in the closest touch with his Department, but never bogged down in its details; that he should know pretty quickly whom he can trust there and whom he should watch with his best weather eye. But just as all discoveries, both in the natural and in the social sciences, are made at the boundaries of a subject, and not at its centre, so a good Cabinet Minister will be constantly watching the work of his Department as though he were making a pilot survey, as it were, of its future activities, and be making it in relation to what he knows is happening in other Departments. Thus a Minister of Education ought to have constantly in mind, when issues of school curricula are before him, how badly we lag behind in technology; or a President of the Board of Trade ought to ask himself why it is that the cheaper goods of hire-purchase furnishing shops are among the monuments of ugliness in our time. A wise Foreign Secretary ought not to count it as a victory if the British Council comes so largely under his jurisdiction; he ought rather to ask why the picture of Great Britain painted in words that are heard only is so much more influential than anything his Council representative in Paris or Rome or Prague seems able to achieve; and perhaps, even more, he ought to give a Saturday afternoon three or four times a year to thinking out, both with his own officials and those of the B.B.C., what may be the influence on international relations of the probability that within ten to fifteen years some events shown by television in London may well be seen in Moscow or Mombasa. I venture also to guess that the first-rate Chancellor of the Exchequer will always be aware of two things: first, that if we have the good fortune to find another Keynes in the next generation, he should be given the freedom of the Treasury and welcomed there with some frequency in

M

order that he may put its chief officials, and even their august chief, through the kind of cross-examination upon forward-looking policy that is the equivalent of that searching combination of questions and dogmas that made Keynes perhaps the greatest British thinker in the field of political economy since Adam Smith; and, second, that he should never leave a young official who shows signs of imagination and the power to take risks in any part of the Establishment Branch of the Treasury for more than five years at the maximum. So, also, a Secretary, of State for the Colonies who wants it said of him, say half a century from now, that he had grasped the real cause of the grave demographic problems of East Africa, would look with serious concern upon officials who, when they were asked to find for him economists who could aid a Governor here, a High Commissioner there, to help in planning the best uses of some colony's resources, recommended to him men whom even the slightest acquaintance would reveal as among the last-ditch defenders of a system of *laissez-faire*. It is really not less important to take measures against the dangers of hunger in the next generation than it is to develop the standards even of so important an institution as Makerere.

Mr. Amery speaks with great emphasis of the burden of Departmental duties, and much of the strength of his case for the change in the structure of the Cabinet that he recommends rests upon the assumption that a Minister in charge of a great Department has no time to think beyond the range of its duties. Quite obviously Mr. Amery here speaks with an authority to which no merely academic observer can pretend. I have no claim to differ from his point except the brief glimpse into these mysteries twice vouchsafed to me when it fell to my lot for two periods, lasting altogether for rather less than three years, to "devil" for two eminent Cabinet Ministers and thus not only to read and annotate their papers but also to see them practically every day during that time. I agree at once that when a big Bill is in the making, and when, especially after the Committee Stage, it is on its way through the House, the burden laid on the Minister is heavy indeed, especially where, as with the Insurance Act of 1911, or that of 1946, each clause is a complicated trap, the dangers of which it takes intense effort to avoid. But, much as I admire the skill of Mr. Amery's argument, I believe that here he has been led into unconscious exaggeration by his anxiety to make a case. Certainly, it is possible to name a very considerable number of Ministers since 1906, who, despite the burden of a great Department, were able to take their full share of Cabinet discussion upon much wider themes, and were not content to sit as silent listeners to debates which did not directly concern their own little plot of garden. That was obviously true of Mr. Lloyd George and of Mr. Churchill; it was true of Lord Haldane and Mr. Neville Chamberlain; it was true of the late Mr. Arthur Henderson and of Lord Samuel; I will not make a catalogue of names except to insist that were such a catalogue made it would inevitably include the name of Mr. Amery himself. That there have been, and, indeed, still are, Ministers to whom the toil of wading through the mass of papers most officials like to thrust before their political chiefs exhausts what energy of mind they have I do not for one moment question; just as I would accept without discussion the shattering physical costs to Ministers of any prolonged period of crisis. But I think that Mr. Amery would himself agree that his own view is limited by three considerations. First, the offices of Prime Minister, Foreign Secretary, and Chancellor of the Exchequer must normally be judged by criteria different in kind from those applied to other Departments; second, it is obviously true that much depends upon the temperament of a Minister—there are those who know how to rest, when to delegate, how to retain a reserve of energy, how to move swiftly through the long-winded memoranda often thrust unnecessarily upon them, just as there are those who cannot delegate, who are bound to meddle with things of minor importance, and (by no means the smallest class) those who literally read at so slow a pace that they fall into dependence upon a skilful private secretary or, as for so many years in the Post Office, into the clutches of an arrogant and masterful Permanent Secretary like the late Sir Evelyn Murray, who shaped so many Postmasters-General to his outlook until he was broken by his failure to realise either the depth of Sir Kingsley Wood's ambition or his determination that no will should over-rule his own at St. Martins-le-Grand. There is an interesting story to be told of the speed and decision with which Sir Kingsley Wood received the aid of his Prime Minister and of the late Sir Warren Fisher, then Permanent Secretary to the Treasury, in getting Sir Evelyn Murray transferred to the less controversial atmosphere of the Board of Customs.

I agree wholly with Mr. Amery that few parties con-

tain as many as twenty men who can stand the strain and
pressure of Cabinet work for a period of four or five
years, especially when these are marked by the heavy
weight of a responsibility like that of war. Certainly that
was also Mr. Lloyd George's view; and in his memorandum in favour of a Coalition Government which, as I
noted earlier, he put to Mr. Balfour in 1910, this was one
of the grounds upon which he urged it. But I believe
this aspect of the Cabinet problem is best seen from a
different angle. Too many Ministers approach the acceptance of Cabinet office gratified, indeed, at the fulfilment
of a high ambition, but deceiving themselves into the
conviction that they really do not want it, or that they
will be worn out quickly by its responsibilities. Viscount
Grey announced his anxiety to retire to a life devoted to
fly-fishing and bird-watching every year; it is notable
that, despite his avowed dislike of office, he remained
the Foreign Secretary of this country for over eleven
years. The Marquis of Ripon has told us that the day he
resigned office was the happiest of his life; but he admitted
that, very shortly thereafter, he began to miss the pleasur-
able routine of exercising power, and that, within a few
months, he was sketching the outline of some future
Cabinet in which he might hope to place himself in the
post he really desired—an attitude which he presently
combined with the conviction that the Tory Government
then in office was clearly ruining the country. Few people
admit, with the straightforward candour of Mr. Churchill, that they have always enjoyed the exercise of power
that office confers, and have enjoyed nothing so much as
exercising the immense authority of the Prime Minister

in years of acute danger; his allusion to the sense of ease it gave him when he attained that high place at perhaps the greatest crisis in our history will be remembered.

I am convinced that there is here a political phenomenon of considerable importance. It is one of the curious conventions of politics that its practitioners should deny their desire for the power the exercise of which is, in fact, the object of their intense ambition. It is another, and hardly less curious convention, that the politician should insist that he is worn out by his exertions. That insistence is only rarely valid. "As a rule," wrote William James, "men habitually use only a small part of the powers which they actually possess, and which they might use under appropriate conditions." The year of danger in 1940 stimulated hundreds of thousands of people in this country to efforts of which they did not know they were capable. Just as the fact that Parliament has been, traditionally, the "best club" in London, with its tempo set by gentlemen of leisure, who, until almost the other day, thought it wholly natural that the House should not sit on Derby day, so the Minister has been far too frequently accustomed to think that because the written tradition is one of fatigue as an obligation of office, he needs long periods of relaxation; and only too often he regards physical activity as mental effort. The phenomenon has been brilliantly described by William James in the same remarkable essay from which I have already quoted.

"Everyone is familiar", he wrote, "with the phenomenon of feeling more or less alive on different days. Everyone knows that on any given day there are energies slumbering in him which the excitements of that day do not call forth, but which he might display if these were greater. Most of us feel as if a sort of cloud weighed upon us, keeping us below our highest notch of clearness in discernment, sureness in reasoning, or firmness in deciding. Compared with what we ought to be, we are only half awake. Our fires are damped, our draughts are checked. We are making use of only a small part of our possible mental and physical resources . . . to what do the better men owe their escape? And, in the fluctuations which all men feel in their own degree of energising, to what are the improvements due, when they occur? In general terms, the answer is plain: either some unusual stimulus fills them with emotional excitement, or some unusual idea of necessity induces them to make an extra effort of will. Excitements, ideas, and efforts, in a word, are what carry us over the dam." Not the least of my objections to Mr. Amery's scheme of Cabinet reorganisation is the fact that its implications ignore the important truth William James here describes. In politics, above all other areas, where an able man is put in a routine job which he can perform without any call upon his full powers, they will either stale by disuse, or he will feel a sense of frustration for which he compensates in some other way. When in the Coalition Government of 1915 in the first World War, Mr. Churchill was driven from the Admiralty to the futility of the Duchy of Lancaster, his sublimation of his distress took the forms, first, of resigning in order to be actually in the battle itself, and, if more slowly, nevertheless perceptibly, in a steady change of conviction which took him back to the Tory convictions in which he had been brought up, and thence, after much inner unhappiness, back to great office where he rediscovered his natural sense of energetic exhilaration. What this sense of unused capacity can do to a man who combines ability with dominating energy has recently been expressed in what is fundamentally a tragic book, by Lord Reith; obviously, for him, the years since he left the B.B.C., which, despite all his unmistakable faults, he made into the remarkable institution that it is, have been wasted and unhappy years. It is a painful spectacle to watch a man whose administrative gifts are so clearly of a high order, trying to compensate for the bitterness of his frustration by the public exhibition of his wounds.

Mr. Amery's approach seems to me to suffer from the fact that, in a political system like ours, it is really not enough to give to half a dozen men, or even half a score, the "excitements, ideas, and efforts" that will "carry them over the dam". I fear that a confinement of power to so small a group as he proposes offers to the Tadpoles and Tapers of every party a dangerously wide front upon which to operate; and, as in the Coalition Government of Mr. Lloyd George, they would find in the subordinate Minister who either did not feel he had enough to do, or, alternatively, felt bitterly that his exclusion from the inner circle was unjustified, a man who would, sooner or later, lend a ready ear to their schemes and intrigues, and thus devote to their success precisely the effort to which they should have been stimulated by their work in the Government. No one, I am confident, who has seen government from close at hand can doubt that this is so. Certainly, it was fascinating, while Mr. Churchill was Prime Minister, to watch the passionate manœuvres of those who thought they were inadequately placed, or unjustly overlooked, to work themselves into Mr. Churchill's good graces. And perhaps I may add, without indiscretion, that it has been even more fascinating, after that defeat of 1945, which shocked him by its unexpectedness, to watch Mr. Churchill himself, though formally the Leader of the Opposition in the House of Commons, deal with the problems of the day as though he were the permanent Prime Minister of an invisible Government whose duty it was to set the configuration of policy within which Mr. Attlee and his colleagues must organise their activities.

X

AN ALTERNATIVE STRUCTURE

Upon this basis, I should argue that the institutional framework of a Cabinet will be at its best when it is primarily composed of those Ministers whose Departments must necessarily engage the major attention of the House of Commons. Some attention, of course, must be given to the party status of men who do not choose to be in charge of such Departments; and almost every Cabinet is better off for one or two Ministers whose Departmental duties are purely nominal, but who can be trusted either to offer wise general counsel, or to give special help at some point where the weight cast upon a given Minister is too important to be carried by a Parliamentary Under-secretary, and needs to be shared by another Minister whose prestige in the House will satisfy its members that their dignity has been fully consulted. By these criteria the Cabinet, in relation to "those above the line" in Mr. Churchill's phrase, would, apart from the Prime Minister himself, normally consist of the following Members: the Foreign Secretary, the Chancellor of the Exchequer, the Home Secretary, the Secretaries of State for Commonwealth Relations and for the Colonies, the Ministers of Defence, Education, and Agriculture, of Labour and of Health, the President of the Board of Trade, and two Ministers with no or small administrative duties, such as the Lord President of the Council and the Lord Privy Seal. That makes a Cabinet of fourteen members, though it is possible that, with the growth of nationalised industries, a fifteenth Minister will be necessary whose relation to Departments like those of Transport, of Fuel and Power, and of Supply, may come closely to resemble that of the Minister of Defence to the three service Departments. I assume, of course, that such a Cabinet would discuss with Ministers "below the line" any matter in which the work of their Departments was particularly relevant.

It will be noted that I exclude, on this scheme, from the Cabinet the Secretary of State for Scotland, and the Lord Chancellor. The grounds for their exclusion seem to me to be pretty clearly common sense. The presence of the Secretary of State for Scotland has its roots in the sentimentality of nationalism rather than in a felt administrative need. It is rare indeed that the office goes to a first-rate political figure; and he rarely carries as much weight when he is put in the Cabinet as half a dozen of his colleagues who are "below the line". It is, of course, an innovation to suggest the omission of the Lord Chancellor. But my view can, I think, be justified on three grounds. In the first place, he is a judge; and it is wholly undesirable that a judge should play the directly political role of a Minister—and since, secondly, it is clearly unnecessary for him to lead the Government in the House of Lords, the necessity of his being directly acquainted with Cabinet papers does not seem incontestable. The more fully, moreover, his office is examined, the more desirable it appears to create directly a Minister of Justice who need no more be a legal figure than the Secretary of State for War a soldier; indeed, if the urgent need for legal reform is to receive political recognition, a lay Minister of Justice ought to replace the office of Lord Chancellor as speedily as possible. If the view be taken that a separate Ministry for this purpose is unnecessary, there is no reason why all the Lord Chancellor's political and legal administrative work should not be transferred to the Home Office which, functionally, has long experience of dealing with legal work. Granted the history, moreover, of legal reform in this country, it is far more likely to be driven forward by a Minister responsible to the House of Commons than by one whose essential functions are centred in the House of Lords. It is not even necessary, of course, that the speakership of the Lords should be associated with the Woolsack; there have been times when the great seal has been in commission, and the work of the late Lord Donoughmore, as Lord Chairman of Committees, has shown conclusively that a Second Chamber does not require the Lord Chancellor to preside over its sittings. On this basis, moreover, it would be possible, at long last, to reform the whole system of judicial patronage, which still bears on its face the character of the age of Lord Eldon rather than of our own. Certainly, with the possible exception of ecclesiastical appointments, it is difficult to think of any area where the exercise of the patronage power has been performed to less advantage in this country. And if it be said that some Lords Chancellor have been expert administrators, Lord Cairns, for example, or Lord Haldane, I think it is a sufficient answer to say that a man with large qualities in this sphere is far better occupied with a great Department which calls out all his powers of constructive imagination than with one the potentialities of which there is no example of a Lord Chancellor seeking to use in the grand style since the Judicature Act of 1873 shaped the office to its present form.

The authors of the notable Machinery of Government Report of 1918 urged that a Cabinet should consist of twelve members and made a persuasive plea for a more coherent system by which functionally to redistribute their powers. I agree with this plea; for though a good deal has been done in this direction since the first World War, a good deal remains to be done, some of it of quite first-rate importance. A Cabinet of twelve represents the field of administration at the time of Sir Robert Peel, when the work of government covered a far smaller area, some of it much less profoundly than is the case in our own day. I doubt whether the number of Ministers whose associations with the Cabinet ought to be direct and continuous can be reduced to less than fourteen or fifteen without a failure to give their Departments the status that is essential to the proper consideration of their problems. While it is, therefore, tempting, on the analogy of the Minister of Defence, to think it desirable to create a Minister of Production, who oversees, as it were, the Board of Trade, the Ministries of Labour and Agriculture, and, to be logical, the Ministries of Supply and of Works, I think the temptation ought to be resisted even though it would reduce the Cabinet to the size thought desirable by the Haldane Committee. For though all these Ministries deal with problems that are interrelated, and therefore cry out for decisive co-ordination, each of them deals with a different group of people from the others, and has a special character which can be grasped, not by a Minister who is, as it were, the chairman of a Committee of Ministers, but by a political chief who can afford the time and effort required to immerse himself in considerable detail in order to penetrate to the roots of that special character. In an economy, moreover, that seeks to achieve full employment as a continuous, and not as an intermittent, feature of its nature, it is inevitable that the Minister of Labour should be regarded as occupying a pivotal post not subordinate save to the Prime Minister and to the Cabinet as a whole. That will become all the more true as the public sector of industry expands; for the more collectivist the society, the more delicate, and the more vital, become the relations between the Government and the trade unions. It is not merely that it becomes urgent to strengthen the machinery which reduces strikes to a minimum—the prohibition of strikes by law is undesirable in a free society; it is also that the functions, and probably, also, the structure, of trade unions will change in large measure compared with their development in a society which remains steadfastly capitalist in character. A Minister of Labour with real courage and insight could do much to ease the difficulties of this transformation so long as his authority is direct and substantial; once, however, he becomes a subordinate Minister "below the line", and living under the shadow of a Minister of Production, he will lack the status appropriate both to the persuasion and the powers he will require in order to fulfil his function.

A Cabinet such as I have outlined seems to me, therefore, the most appropriate to the conditions we confront. It is small enough to learn to work as a team; given a wise Prime Minister, it need carry no passengers; and it is limited to members whose work requires the status involved in being "above the line". It ought to be added here that all paper schemes are subject to the inevitable limitation that they presuppose the choice by the Prime Minister of men with the capacity and character the work of a Cabinet requires. No one who knows the history of the British Cabinet since the time of the younger Pitt can assume that the Prime Minister will feel free to choose his colleagues on the basis of these presuppositions. He must give close attention to considerations which limit him to the selection of the best possible Ministers in the given circumstances he confronts, not to the selection of the best Ministers he regards as available. He must pay considerable regard to party opinion; there are certain men, even certain interests, a party will expect to see in the Cabinet; and nothing injures the hold of the Prime Minister upon its loyalty so much as when he makes choices the party either dislikes or cannot understand. A Tory Prime Minister who neglected the claims of the ancient land-owning class would rapidly weaken his authority, just as a Labour Prime Minister who neglected the claims of the trade unions to have men who have risen from their ranks to a seat in the House of Commons would inevitably encounter a climate of hostility. It is, indeed, worth noting that the wider the social experience a Cabinet represents, the more firm will be the devotion that it evokes from the party out of which it is made. It is highly probable, for example, that, without the support of Mr. Arthur Henderson, Mr. Asquith would have failed to get the support of the Labour Movement for conscription in the first World War; and, had not Mr. Ernest Bevin been his Minister of Labour, I doubt whether Mr. Churchill could have persuaded the trade unions to accept the direction of labour in the second.

The original choice is of the first importance. It is hardly less clear that the Prime Minister must have the courage swiftly and decisively to call for resignations when it is clear to him that some particular appointment has turned out to be a mistake. It is historically clear that few Prime Ministers do this with the vigour that is required. Sometimes they take refuge in a change of office, even a promotion from one Department to a greater post. Sometimes they shrink from change from fear of offence to the party as a whole, or to some section of it to which an unsatisfactory Minister is closely affiliated. Sometimes a Minister who ought clearly to go is retained on grounds of personal friendship, or because those who are interested in the subject-matter covered by his Department are powerful, and look upon him as the expression of their purposes. There is no graver mistake a Prime Minister can commit than to keep someone in high office of whose unfitness for it he has become genuinely aware. I refrain from dealing with the last decade; that raises issues too delicate to touch upon, though I venture to say quite frankly that both Mr. Churchill and Mr. Attlee have kept Ministers in important offices who made it plain quite early that, whatever their qualities, they were not those required in the political head of a Department. But no one will now seek to deny that when Mr. Neville Chamberlain appointed Sir Thomas Inskip (later Viscount Caldecote) to be Minister for the Co-ordination of Defence he was guilty of a futile appointment which became more futile every day that it was prolonged. Few people would seriously defend Mr. Ramsay MacDonald's choice of the late Lord Londonderry as Secretary of State for Air in his "National" Government. Anyone who looks at the list of names of those who were Ministers of Education from 1931 to 1940 can hardly help being convinced that the three Prime Ministers involved thought it a Department of quite secondary importance to which might be relegated Ministers who had failed in other Departments. I will not say that the outcome of their view is the immense gap in our national intellectual equipment revealed in 1946 by the Barlow Report, for the gap was already wide when, in admissible deference to the fantastic Geddes Committee of 1921, Mr. Lloyd George threw overboard the Education Act of 1918; and it is probably true to say that the Education Act of 1902 was already overdue by fifteen or twenty years. My point may perhaps be best put in the famous phrase of Mr. Gladstone that "a Prime Minister must be a good butcher". Once he decides to temper the wind to the shorn lamb, there is little reason to suppose that his own weaknesses as Prime Minister will not be costly to the nation.

There is one final thing that it is perhaps worth while to emphasise. People who are obsessed with the immensity of our problems, the far greater range they cover than was the case in Bagehot's time, and the higher responsibility of seeking answers to them, when, perhaps, above all, there seems to be perpetual crisis everywhere, and the need for emergency action every day, are always calling for a Cabinet of all the talents, and bemoaning the fact that no one can look at any recent Government without the realisation that few of its members have possessed the exceptional qualities we call genius. I should like to say with all the force I can that Cabinets of all the talents are rarely durable institutions. A Cabinet can stand one Mr. Lloyd George, or one Mr. Churchill, the kind of statesman of whom it is immediately obvious that he will see into most things, dominate most discussions, and hold the public opinion outside as one of his instruments inside. It was much the same with both the elder and the younger Pitt, and, obviously, with Mr Gladstone.

I do not myself think that any Cabinet can carry more than one of such men. What the modern Cabinet needs, save in times of supreme urgency like a war, is the man of solid sense, anxious to be enterprising, ready to take the risk of being courageous, dependable, and unselfish. He

N

ought not, generally, to cultivate the rhetorical side of his subject, so that all he has to say seems an effort to scale the heights of oratory. He ought not to have an ardour for applause. He needs to have that gift of patient labour which gets through a heavy load of work without a groan at the burden he has to bear. He ought to realise that, as a Minister, he is not there for the rest of his life, and that his main business is, on one side, that of taking the initiative, and, on the other, that of co-ordination of the big affairs. He must be able to refuse consideration of minor points which his officials ought to decide for themselves. He must be able to keep cool, and to be angry only as a matter of calculated policy. He must know how to explain what his Department is doing, and to make what it is doing interesting to the public as well as to Parliament. He must have the capacity, as it were, to stand upon an eminence, and see the affairs of his Department in a full perspective. He needs, of course, to be a good judge of men, able to persuade them to follow him, so that his right to command seems always a reserve power upon which he rarely needs to draw. Lastly, I think the one thing of all things he should be able to avoid is the creation of a routine of habit through which none of his colleagues can discern a clear thread of policy; and as he reflects upon what makes up that policy, he should never lose a sense of respect for humble men, and should seek, as an inescapable obligation, that precision in the use of words which is so often an index to precision in the ideas which lie behind the words. The one unforgivable thing in a modern Cabinet Minister is the possession of the vague and shapeless mind that is incapable of giving a pattern of thought to the facts he has constantly to consider and reconsider. For a Minister who cannot form a pattern of thought cannot, either, form a pattern of decision. It is urgent for us always to remember that the Cabinet is a committee of men who have to find their way from an agreed plane of thought to an agreed plane of action, and to make their road, after every public criticism has exhausted itself, one down which the citizens of a country march willingly without any fear that the grim alternative is the concentration camp and the predetermined trial.

PART THREE
THE CIVIL SERVICE

XI
THE CIVIL SERVICE IN THE TWENTIETH CENTURY

NEVER during the whole course of the nineteenth century did our Civil Service have to face tests as heavy or as disorganising as the Civil Service of the twentieth, which, with but half its span closed, has already had to meet the challenge of two world wars, and has, as yet, been unable to move to that area of activity where it can think out the problems pressed upon it without that strain of nerve which comes from the fear that there is no assurance of a lasting peace. It is the least that can be said of the Civil Service which, by the Order in Council of 1870, Mr. Gladstone built upon the Trevelyan-Northcote Report of 1853, that, by 1914, it had become loyal, efficient, uncorrupted, and that it continuously attracted to its ranks some of the ablest minds in the country. The year 1914 showed that it was capable of swift adaptation, and that, within a fairly broad framework of principles, it was usually willing both to be critical of itself and open to experiment. It had, of course, its weaknesses. The Treasury still combined a profound acumen with a deep suspicion of anything that tended to the building of a positive state. The Foreign Office never lost its essential character as a nest of aristocratic singing-birds, mainly hatched out at Eton, and only occasionally dragged out of an obsolete Whig tradition by the passionate determination of a man like Sir Eyre Crowe. The Colonial Office, having come to the conclusion that, in Disraeli's famous phrase, "our wretched colonies" need not be regarded as "millstones round our necks", had become, if not Charles Buller's immortal "Mr. Mother Country", at least a spinsterish aunt with a somewhat peevish conviction that the nephews and nieces must never change except in terms of her special inspiration. The professional soldiers at the War Office, and nearly all the professional sailors who formed the Board of Admiralty, were, all of them, above all in the context of the new air weapon, remarkable illustrations of what Clemenceau really meant by his cynical aphorism that war is too important a matter to be left to the generals and the admirals.

It had a number of general weaknesses. It was much too rigidly hierarchical, much too convinced that a man who could get a First Class in "Greats" at Oxford could see all the problems of his time with an insight and imagination less likely to be available to other men. It had small interest in science, and even smaller interest in technology. Its leading officials only too rarely looked beyond the ranks of the administrative class with the hope that first-class ability might be discovered there. They accepted, without undue resistance, not only the abominably low salaries the Treasury imposed upon them; what was perhaps worse, they resented the effort of the trade unions in the Civil Service to ask for higher pay and, generally speaking, it does not seem ever seriously to have occurred to them that men and women in the lower grades who, once they had reached their maximum, had nothing before them but the prospect of a dull routine from which only retirement could redeem them, would not thereby be stimulated by the zeal and devotion which their own possession of immense influence and high responsibility so often evoked. With notable exceptions, it is not easy to answer the charge made, in the light of his own experience, by one who had been eminent amongst them but had chosen a new path to self-fulfilment. "If you read an official file, especially a file on a new project," wrote Sir Michael Sadler in 1932, "you will find as a rule that the experienced official is better at telling a subordinate what *not* to do than at interesting him in ways of doing better what is already passably well done, or encouraging him to conceive bold innovations in existing methods of administration. Hence there is a tone in these public services which is discouraging to novelty, an atmosphere of birth-control restrictive of new beginnings and new growths.... It is Humanism with the sap dried out of it. It is instinctively suspicious of experimental science. It is not prone to economic or scientific research. It prefers to deal with things in symbols or in words alone, and is not in the habit of going to see things or places or processes before it puts into words a critical judgment upon them."

Nevertheless, it must be admitted that, despite these weaknesses, the Civil Service of 1914 made a contribution of overwhelming importance to victory in the first World War. Not least in that contribution was the work of some of the younger civil servants who were sent to create or to develop during its course some of the new

Departments it became necessary to establish—Food, for instance, and Munitions, Shipping, and Labour. But, from the Treaty of Versailles down to the end of the second World War, it is far from easy to escape from the judgment of Sir Michael Sadler that I have quoted. The reason for this is, I think, important. The Civil Service which functioned so remarkably in the first World War was fashioned for a society the foundations of which were, in fact, destroyed in the War they helped so largely to win. While it is true that the service was reorganised after 1919, that new changes were made in its structure, that Whitleyism was introduced, that new means of entering the Foreign Office and the Diplomatic and Consular services were devised, even that a considerable number of officials were promoted from the lower grades to the administrative class, the novelty in form certainly did not find a proportionate novelty in spirit. It is quite true that Whitehall, with but a few exceptions, remained incorruptible, independent, and, again with but a few exceptions, loyal. But if the high permanent officials ever suspected they were plunged into a new world, there is little that they ever did to show that they were aware of it.

They never met, with any imaginative insight, the problems of a society with never less than one million unemployed, and, more often, as many as two millions and more. They never pushed forward the plans so urgently needed for the re-equipment of industry, and for the development of greater efficiency, on the side of labour as well as on that of management. They did astonishingly little to bring science and technology into partnership with industry and agriculture. They showed no sense of the urgent need for education at a far higher level than obtained, with the consequences so gravely revealed—to take but one example—in the Barlow *Report on Scientific Manpower*. They did not compel attention to the very serious problem of monopolies, price-fixing, the organisation of scarcity. Save for the brief period when Mr. John Wheatley was Minister of Health, they did not press the Cabinet into any serious grasp either of the scale of the housing problem or of the impossibility of leaving it to be dealt with by private enterprise. A considerable percentage of teachers, both men and women, was either half-trained, or not trained at all; and the level of salaries paid, even after the increases decided upon by the Burnham Committee, made most really able young men and women think of teaching as among the least desirable careers open to them when the choice came to be made. They knew that there were thousands of classes so large that it was impossible for the children in them to be seriously educated, just as they knew that an education which ends at fourteen stops just at the point where, save for the most exceptional children, its creative consequences begin; yet it is not easy to find in the then Board of Education any sense of anxiety about these and other related questions of high importance. After the first big effort at reorganisation, indeed, in 1919–20, it is difficult to feel that the heads of the Civil Service showed anything like the imagination and drive that were required even for its own adjustment to the claims of the new society produced by the great World War. Whitleyism, after its first five years, became little more than a machine for dealing with wage, and similar,

claims, and for safeguarding, as far as possible, the rights
of seniority in the processes of promotion; it realised little
of the hopes it had roused about post-entry training, the
search for new talent in the lower grades, or the effort to
encourage the lower officials in the hierarchy to contri-
bute their ideas to the common pool of administrative
effort. Not all the devotion the Civil Service brought to
its work was a compensation for the absence of imaginative enterprise on its part at a time when this quality was
vital to the national future.

It is no answer to this view to say that the civil servant
is concerned with administration, that it is for his Minister to take the initiative in policy. Everyone with the
least acquaintance with government cannot but be
aware that there is a give and take between every Minister and his chief officials which makes the latter unseen
partners, as it were, in the purposes he seeks to implement.
If one takes the Foreign Office, for example, it is difficult
to believe that, except for the two years when Mr.
Arthur Henderson was Foreign Secretary, there was any
sustained or massive effort to bring the League of Nations
into effective life. The main objective of the Treasury, in
concert with the Bank of England, seemed to be a return,
whatever the price, to the gold standard; and it fought
with obstinate determination to prevent any Chancellor
of the Exchequer from being beguiled into any serious
consideration of those heresies of Lord Keynes through
which, as Professor Pigou has noted, economists all over
the world were awakened from their dogmatic slumbers.
Anyone who reads the report, and the evidence, of the
Royal Commission on the West Indies, completed just

as the second World War began, is not likely to emerge from the experience with an excessive admiration for the experimentalism of the Colonial Office. So far, indeed, as events themselves permitted, *quieta non movere* seems to have been the mood in which the civil servants in the highest class approached problems the very greatness of which ought to have stimulated them to exciting innovation. Even if one holds that, with but few exceptions, they were never led by Ministers anxious to experiment on the large scale, the evidence points to the conclusion that they made but little effort to push them towards that anxiety. Taken as a whole, the Civil Service of the inter-war years showed a lack of courage, an absence of profound conviction, an anxiety to criticise rather than to create, which well corresponds to Sir Michael Sadler's jibe—"humanism with the sap dried out of it". A generation which needed men with the vigour and drive of Chadwick, Rowland Hill, Kay-Shuttleworth, Eyre Crowe, did not find them. There was plenty of high competence, as in Sir Warren Fisher or Sir John Anderson, in Sir Richard Hopkins or Lord Tyrrell; there was plenty of deep devotion. What the Civil Service suffered from in the inter-war years was an anxiety to return to what the late American President Harding called "normalcy" without any realisation that "normalcy" meant exactly those pre-1914 conditions which the war had rendered obsolete.

That becomes the more clear if one compares the atmosphere of Whitehall in the nineteen-thirties with the atmosphere of Washington under the New Deal. No doubt there was much that was rugged, imperfect, inefficient under the Roosevelt Administration. But the atmosphere was exciting. There were great adventures afoot, and most of the young men who went there were filled with the sense that they were part of them. The efforts of the W.P.A., under Mr. Harry Hopkins, would, I am certain, have terrified the Treasury. But they gave back to many hundred thousands of workers a renewed sense of self-respect; they saved them from that tragic conviction of futility which was one of the main trage-dies of unemployment in the distressed areas of this coun-try. It was, moreover, a heartening thing to realise that unemployment among intellectuals, the artist, the actor, the writer, the architect, could be used for social purposes. The W.P.A. theatre took the drama into places where no one had ever seen a theatre before. Architects and builders co-operated in creating a number of admirable buildings, of which the superb open-air theatre at Boulder Dam is only one outstanding example. Much was done for music and for the development of mural art. The W.P.A. guides produced a survey of the forty-eight states which, both geographically and historically, is a model of what such things should be. The development of electric power, moreover, was not only of immense value to the United States; some of the work done in this field, above all in the creation of the famous Tennessee Valley Authority, is likely to become the basis of world-wide experiment in the future. It all, of course, meant taking risks, making mistakes, going down a road which led to a jungle from which the President and his advisers had to hack their way out again. But, despite all of this, it had two results worth all the taxation it involved, and the deficits in the budget which so terrified the bankers and the old-fashioned economists. It made government a positive thing, instead of the unhappy and uneasy negation it had been from 1921 to 1932; and it gave people, quite ordinary people, an interest in the processes of politics which, war apart, they had not possessed since the death of Lincoln. No doubt it secured for Mr. Roosevelt a depth of hatred from his opponents which equalled, if it did not surpass, the anger evoked against Jefferson and Jackson. But it also secured for him a volume of enthusiastic support which makes it fair to say that there is a very real sense in which, if Mr. Truman is in office, Mr. Roosevelt nevertheless remains in power.

It is, no doubt, true to say that the three or four top civil servants in an American government department are mostly birds of passage, who stay there with a President whom they support, and go out of office with him. The British civil servant, on the other hand, has chosen a life career, and must learn to adapt himself to Cabinets of very different political complexions. I do not doubt the importance of this difference, though I think we must be careful not to exaggerate its consequences. The high official in this country maintains, on the whole, a loyalty to the decisions of any Minister he serves. That does not for one moment mean that he is lacking in strong views about the policy his Department should follow, or that he will not make every effort in his power to persuade his Minister to accept his views. He will always give way when the Minister has finally put his foot down; but he is unlikely to give way until that moment is reached. Only too often, moreover, his Minister may be someone who knows little or nothing about the work of his Department, in which case his policy is pretty sure to reflect the outlook of his chief officials. Or the Minister may come with some quite general principle he wishes to embody in a Bill; in instances of this kind his chief officials are normally in a position to set the limits within which he can be persuaded that his principle can usefully operate. And a strong-minded civil servant who is anxious to prevent a timid Minister from embarking upon experiments on any major scale has almost always the power in his hands to arrest any effort for change if the desire to do something flits uneasily across the Minister's mind.

There are some simple illustrations of all this. Once Mr. Attlee had made up his mind that Indian independence was both desirable and necessary he was fully supported by the India Office, though I do not suppose his policy was approved by any of the major civil servants there. Mr. Ernest Bevin was an outstanding Minister of Labour in Mr. Churchill's War Cabinet. When he became Foreign Secretary in Mr. Attlee's Government, he entered a Department with many of the problems of which he was wholly unacquainted. Among these, the problem of Palestine was outstanding, though it was one upon which, in his presence, and without his opposition, his party, at the Blackpool Conference only a few weeks before he took office, had outlined a policy unanimously, and in quite explicit terms. The Labour Party's policy was the direct antithesis of the policy upon Palestine held by the Foreign Office ever since the Balfour Declaration of 1916; and, year by year from that date, the officials of the Foreign Office had been building, piece by piece, ways and means of narrowing the implications of the Mandate of 1922 to the narrowest possible area; that was why it had sponsored the creation of the Arab League, why it had created a Transjordan of which it was in virtually complete control, since its ruler, Abdullah, not only depended upon a British subsidy, but had an army trained and commanded by British officers, and that was why finally, in the spring of 1939, Mr. Malcolm MacDonald, then the Colonial Secretary in the Chamberlain Government, had imposed the notorious White Paper which not only deprived the Mandate of its meaning, but was the subject of a Labour vote of censure in the House of Commons, moved by Mr. Herbert Morrison, supported in a passionate speech of indignant protest by Mr. Philip Noel-Baker, and was attacked by Mr. Churchill, Lord Cecil, and Mr. Amery, all of whom had helped to make the Mandate in 1922, and had been its strong supporters ever since. I will not go into the motives which led the Foreign Office to support Arab hostility to the growth of a Jewish Palestine with all its strength. All I am here concerned to do is to point out that, within less than a month of becoming Foreign Secretary, Mr. Ernest Bevin had not only adopted wholeheartedly the view of his officials—for which, also, he secured the strong support of the Cabinet, and an overwhelming backing from the Parliamentary Labour Party—but that he imposed it upon Palestine with a fierce intensity that practically made it into occupied territory controlled by some 90,000 British troops virtually engaged in a continuous guerrilla warfare with the Jews. I am quite confident that neither the Parliamentary Party, nor the Cabinet, nor, indeed, Mr.

Bevin himself, had any idea that he would "stake his reputation" on the success of his policy when he became Foreign Secretary, though, of course, the responsibility both for the attempt to implement it, and for its disastrous failure, is the collective responsibility of the Cabinet. But the whole affair is an extraordinary example of the power of officials to get their political chief not only to accept their point of view, but also to impose it with relentless fury until it became obvious that its application was injuring the good name of Great Britain all over the world. No one can examine even the incomplete documentation we have upon this issue without realising that the major source of Mr. Bevin's decisions was the profound conviction of a small group of his officials that the time had come finally to undo a policy which it was the tradition of the Department to insist should never have been adopted.

I take this case because, as everyone knows, Mr. Bevin is an astute and determined man who is normally more accustomed to lead than to be led. My third illustration concerns the power of officials over a new Minister who came to his Department with no special policy, and was, above everything, a cautious person determined to take no risks which might jeopardise his reputation for being a sound and safe man. When Mr. Ramsay MacDonald took office for the second time, he offered my late colleague, Mr. H. B. Lees-Smith, then member of Parliament for Keighley, the choice between the Post Office and the Department of Overseas Trade. Mr. Lees-Smith did me the honour of asking my advice upon his choice; and I unhesitatingly urged upon him the wisdom of taking the Post Office, largely upon the ground that it offered a wide field for administrative experiment without the need to ask Parliament for any large-scale legislation. Mr. Lees-Smith agreed, and we spent a good deal of time compiling from official and unofficial sources a list of possible measures which we thought would be desirable and attractive. Under the then organisation of the Post Office, its Permanent Secretary was the late Sir Evelyn Murray, who may, I think, be fairly described as belonging spiritually to the era of Lord Melbourne when to get things left alone was a supreme object of official policy. Mr. Lees-Smith sent for Sir Evelyn Murray and suggested that they discuss the list of proposed changes when the Permanent Secretary had spent a few days in thinking over what the changes would involve. About a week later, Mr. Lees-Smith had lunch with me and explained that, for the present, he did not think the time was ripe for Post Office reform.

What had happened? When Sir Evelyn Murray went back to discuss the list with Mr. Lees-Smith he had begun with a formidable preamble. The Post Office was a highly complex Department, very easily open to criticism because it was in touch with the public at a hundred points. It had already many new and heavy burdens to bear, above all, perhaps, its responsibility for the B.B.C., and the need to secure the right decision upon the future of beam wireless, for the projection of which its own engineers were largely responsible. He felt that these two problems already exposed the Postmaster-General to important discussions in the House of Commons, as well as with the outside interests affected, and these would, no doubt, absorb a good deal of the Minister's time. He pointed out, further, to Mr. Lees-Smith that the very complexity of the Post Office made it desirable that he should make himself thoroughly acquainted with the details of its existing organisation before he embarked upon changes which would need the most careful consideration before they were adopted, above all thinking out ways of preventing them from being unpopular either with special interests, or with the public generally, and thus leading certainly to a spate of questions, even to debate, and, it might well be, an attack upon Mr. Lees-Smith's first Estimates in the House of Commons. He therefore urged upon Mr. Lees-Smith the wisdom of spending the first eighteen months or so upon the hard job of knowing the Department intimately; then, Sir Evelyn urged, Mr. Lees-Smith would be ready to attempt large-scale changes with real confidence. Since Mr. Lees-Smith was a cautious man by temperament, he thought the Permanent Secretary's advice quite admirable, with the result that his name is not associated with any major measures of social reform. It is significant that when, a little later, the ambitious and hustling Sir Kingsley Wood arrived at St. Martin's-le-Grand one of the first steps he took was to arrange for the transference of Sir Evelyn Murray from the Post Office to the Board of Customs and Excise, where his philosophy of administration was less likely to obstruct experiment.

o

XII

THE ADMINISTRATIVE CLASS

If I may be dogmatic, I should like to say that, broadly speaking, the work of the permanent civil servants at the top of the hierarchy was far less creative in the second World War than in the first. There are, of course, notable exceptions and, though it is invidious to pick out names, I should like to say here that both from what I know and from what I have heard from those who knew far more than I can do, the achievement of Sir Edward Bridges, the present Permanent Secretary to the Treasury, is one of the most outstanding records of the war. But, by and large, the temporary civil servants at the top level, who were recruited for war-time only, though, happily, some of them have remained on in a permanent capacity, did a far more remarkable job than the officials who were immersed in traditional experience. Again, it would be invidious to pick out names, but I cannot resist the temptation to note the remarkable career of Sir Oliver Franks who went, as everyone knows, from the study of logic to become one of the most skilful negotiators the Civil Service has ever possessed. And it is no more than their due to emphasise the immense credit Mr. Attlee and Mr. Bevin deserve when they chose that subtle and gracious mind to succeed Lord Inverchapel as British Ambassador to Washington.

What are the outstanding lessons of the second World War from the angle of the Civil Service? There are four to which I should like to draw quite special attention. The first is the need to recruit a considerable number of men and women into the service at an age which may vary from thirty to forty, and to give them, from the outset, highly responsible work at a level which begins close to that which marks the work of an Assistant Under-secretary of State. There is evidence and to spare that Whitehall would greatly benefit by being exposed, on a reasonable scale, to the ideas and experience of men and women who have, for anything from ten to twenty years of their adult life, been in some entirely different career from that of the normal entrant to the Civil Service. It may be business or trade unionism, finance or academic life, one or other of the services; I am confident that nothing but good would result from drawing officials from sources like these. They would bring in a new point of view, they would compel refreshing examination of tra-ditional ways, they would relate the Department to which they went to a new audience whose voice it is always good for the official to hear. It would not be necessary in every case to ask new entrants of this type to bind them-selves to a life's career. I think there is everything to be said for making possible periods of service that may be as short as three years or five or ten, or engagement to assist in the fulfilment of some special project a Department has in view. The supreme example of the kind of rela-tionship I have in mind is, of course, that of the late Lord Keynes. Agree or disagree with either his theories, or with some of the decisions to which he persuaded the Treasury, I think no one who worked with him there but would agree that he was like a new wind blowing through rooms where too many men for too many years had been chained to a system of dogmas they had come to regard as eternal truths. His remarkable combination of profound analytic power, capacity for persuasive argument, and a certain impish wit which never excluded a sensitive regard for other people's opinions, made him, in his Treasury period, of a value to the nation it would be difficult to overestimate. I agree, of course, that a man of Keynes' stature comes only once or twice in a generation. My anxiety is to be sure that men in whom there is something of his quality are brought into Whitehall, are indeed looked for by Whitehall, as a normal part of its everyday effort to get the capacity proportionate to its task.

Here, of course, I speak of the administrative class only. And it is of this class that I am anxious to venture upon two other suggestions. The first is a doubt whether their contacts, as officials, are wide enough, not merely within this country itself, but also outside its boundaries. Few things have impressed me more than the immense value, during the war, of direct and constant discussions between our own civil servants and those of the American Government, and those of the Governments in exile, from 1940 to 1945. If I may hazard a speculation about the differences between them, I should have said that the Americans were younger, and had more vitality than British officials, and that it was far easier to develop understanding and friendship with the Norwegians, the Belgians, and the French, more or less in that order, than with some of our officials. Few of the foreign civil servants had the same eager quest for perfection as ours, but most of them, especially the Americans and the Norwegians, were far more anxious to know how our system worked than we were to know how their different systems worked. Some notable exceptions apart, it was easier for the ordinary citizen like myself to discuss common interests in public administration with the Norwegians, the French, or the Belgians, than it was with our own people; I add that this was especially true if one compares the American Embassy and the foreign offices of the exiled Governments with the social climate of our own Foreign Office. Taking the over-all picture, I feel fairly confident that it is an accurate generalisation to say that there was a greater barrier between the general body of our own citizens and the higher officials than there was between the higher officials of the Governments in exile and either their citizens or our own; and subsequent journeys abroad have more than ever convinced me that this is the case. I must add that what I have said of foreign officials is not less true of Commonwealth officials also.

Over a decade ago, my colleague, Professor W. A. Robson, pointed out that the most obvious assumption upon which the British Civil Service is based is that it "should be divided into categories which reflect, if they do not reproduce, the social structure and economic inequalities of our society". Since he wrote, a retired official of some eminence, Mr. H. E. Dale, has actually written a book of which one of the major themes is an emphasis upon this type of division, and the expression of an emerging regret that the tendency of the time is, on the whole, against the maintenance of the division based upon such categories. I wholeheartedly agree with Professor Robson that "this system has served its purpose and will prove definitely obstructive unless it is severely modified". It is not only, as he says, that students from universities other than Oxford and Cambridge ought not to find themselves handicapped by the examination for entrance into the administrative class. It is not even the anomaly, to which he draws attention, that there are now few, if any, great political positions not open to men and women of working-class origin, while the main body of the chief officials still come from a fairly narrow class area which educational reconstruction will still leave fairly narrow for at least something like twenty years from now. Both of these are evil, because they really mean that the full grasp of the assumptions upon which legislation implying radical change is based tends for most high officials to be purely intellectual, and to lack the emotional drive behind it which makes co-operation between the Minister and his chief permanent officials loyal on a much more formal plane than when the departure from traditional policy is pretty small or even hardly existent. The late John Wheatley would not have driven his great housing measure through in 1924 if he had not been the kind of Minister who drives his Department relentlessly to the goal he has chosen. When Mr. Churchill was Home Secretary in 1911 his personal initiative and energy were the sources of that beneficent change which abolished the awful rule of solitary confinement for a period in a convicted man's prison term. I add, with respectful regret, that I have rarely known a British embassy or legation abroad where there was any real insight into, or organised relations with, the people who did not belong to the official hierarchy or to the "best families", and that, with of course exceptions, this has continued after 1945. Or, to take another example, no permanent officials in the Lord Chancellor's Department have ever urged upon him the need to overhaul thoroughly a legal system the foundations of which have not been scrutinised *au fond* since the time of Bentham. And one would have thought that officials of the Ministry of Labour, especially in the distressed areas during the inter-war years, would have gone back to their different Ministers to represent with passion that the men and women, even young persons, whom they saw in those endless queues before the Labour Exchanges could not be left to rot at street corners, usually month after month, and not seldom year after year. But passionate indignation is a luxury not provided for in the conventional code of the official's behaviour; that is why the Civil Service showed, in so many of the fields where a positive policy was called for, so undesirable a combination of critical hostility and half-conscious obstruction. And, in the diplomatic service, do not let us forget that, while Sir Nevile Henderson regarded his appointment to Berlin as the direct action of Providence, I can think of only one *diplomat de carrière* who went to Moscow with the unbreakable resolution to break through the so-called "Iron Curtain".

Professor Robson rightly rules out from consideration any introduction of a "spoils" system into the environment of Whitehall. He pins his hopes on what he describes as "the change in ambition among the younger generation, from a desire to make as much money as possible to a desire to do work which is both interesting in itself and informed by a definite social purpose—provided, of course, that a reasonable standard of living is attached thereto". I am, I fear, less optimistic in this regard than Professor Robson. He is undoubtedly right whenever it is a matter of handling a great crisis—the war, for example, or the New Deal in the days before Park Avenue and Beacon Hill began to realise that President Roosevelt was not merely restoring its lost confidence to America, but presenting it to the felt necessities of the twentieth century. But I am not so certain that Professor Robson is right as to periods where there is no crisis. I have been, quite frankly, dismayed by the salaries offered to, sometimes demanded by, the major figures in the new nationalised industries. I can well believe that the chief officials in the Trade Union and Co-operative Movements, in a body like the Labour Party, or the Government Departments are paid too little. But I do not see any reason why a civil servant nearing the retiring age, when he becomes a member of the central board of a nationalised industry, should receive nearly double the salary he received as a Permanent Secretary, or why the General Secretary of a trade union, similarly elevated, should receive four to five times his previous salary, and about eight times as much as a director of the Co-operative Wholesale Society; nor do I think that part-time members of regional boards should be paid for work that, as members of local authorities, they do free of charge for the power and dignity of the office; and I can find no logic behind the decision to pay the chairman of the Coal Board, or of the Electricity Board, almost twice as much as the Permanent Secretary of the Treasury will receive if and when the scales recommended by the Chorley Committee come into operation. *Mutatis mutandis*, it is much the same all the way down the line between the nationalised industries, on the one hand, and the Civil Service, on the other. When the argument is used that we could not get the men we want except at these high salaries, I think we are getting to the boundaries of the absurd. We are allowing the standards of the City to evoke exactly the hopes that are most undesirable among the men and women who, in the admirable phrase Professor Robson quotes from H. G. Wells, by becoming public officials "have put adventures in gain behind them". In my own view, too much of the spirit of the City has invaded Whitehall, and it is wholly undesirable, especially as the publicly owned sector of industry increases, to make responsible officials set their standards of living by those of men on the verge of the plutocracy with its habits of what Veblen called "conspicuous waste". These standards may easily prove fatal to the evocation of that imaginative understanding both of their own subordinates and of the workers as a whole if the mental climate of Whitehall is adjusted to the Britain of *The Tatler* and *The Sketch* when the official goes home at the end of his day.

The second important matter implicit, as I think, both in the inter-war years, and even during the war itself, is the excessive sense, in too many of the chief permanent officials, of being a special caste distinguished by the possession of knowledge and insight which ordinary mortals, even all but the most eminent of politicians, cannot hope to share. This has emerged in a number of ways. Partly, it can be seen in the very phrasing of the official documents; Mr. Churchill's demand for direct and forthright statement—which, incidentally, resulted in the production of Sir Ernest Gowers' superb pamphlet *Plain Words*—was born of nothing so much as the weariness of a man accustomed to making swift decisions on important issues with civil servants who wanted above everything to safeguard themselves from the horror of making a mistake. It can be seen again in the zest for uniformity, the precedent becoming a Procrustes' bed to which all proposed novelties must be adjusted. It emerges in the anxiety to build Royal Commissions, so far as possible, of men and women who can, on the whole, be counted upon to give vent only to views which to the Civil Service seem safe and sound; even under the Labour Government of 1945 the cases were rare when, save by accident, a vigorous personality was chosen of whom it was known that he or she would take an independent line. No one can read Mr. R. H. S. Crossman's book on the Anglo-American Commission on Palestine without realising that, by the time the Commission reported, he had been noted in Whitehall as a trouble-maker whom it would be unwise to use again in a similar way. Nor is it less interesting to note the smooth evasiveness of the Report of the Royal Commission on the Press, so often in patent contradiction with the outcome of the special enquiries it ordered to be made, or the careful limitation of the terms of reference for the Royal Commission on the Death Penalty so that its outcome would cause the least possible difficulty afterwards for the Home Office. In general, moreover, most of the problems confronted by Whitehall are too often encountered indirectly as papers to be read, and far too little as visual contacts directly experienced. Certainly, a good trade union official had a far more realistic grasp of what it was like to stand in a queue at the Labour Exchange, especially in small towns, than the men in Whitehall who were responsible for their supervision. I was myself greatly impressed by the comment of a trade union official with whom I visited a number of the area offices of the Ministry of National Insurance where there was an air of spaciousness and comfort: "That's not the Civil Service," he said, "that's Jim Griffiths telling them what he wants done and seeing that they do it." I do not forget the way in which the Post Office and the Colonial Office send their head-quarters officials into the field as part of their training. But it would be good to know that there was an inter-change between the chief administrative officers of local authorities and the men in Whitehall who pass judg-ment on their proposals. It would be better if the chief officials at the Ministry of Education sent their children, say for one year, to the less adequate council schools and compared the effect upon them of being units in classes which may contain upwards of forty children with the effect of being at ease in Zion in classes at St. Paul's or Westminster or Winchester or Eton. Far too much official experience is so indirect that it fails to be suffi-ciently pungent to evoke an emotional response—a healthy anger, for example, or the kind of ruthless drive for some end felt deeply that made Sir Robert Morant not only a deeply hated man but one who, a generation after his death, is still the outstanding symbol of the civil servant who gets things done.

I believe, further, that Whitehall needs to encourage a

far greater mobility among officials, both within the Departmental structure, on the one hand, and between that structure and the outside world, on the other. It is much too easy to make the Civil Service a life career while doing nothing but the just adequate performance of routine functions. It ought not to be necessary, for example, to offer special allowances to members of the Foreign Office who learn Russian or Arabic or Chinese; they ought to be taken by officials in their stride as one way of proving their interest in, and fitness for, their work. It is certain that there is no inconsiderable number of civil servants who feel, after a few years' experience of the Department, that they have chosen the wrong career and would like, if the sacrifice was not too great, to try their luck outside the Civil Service. But if the civil servant discovers this at any age between thirty-four and forty, he might have to lose, in any grade, the pension rights of anything from sixteen to twenty-four years' service. I therefore wholeheartedly agree with Professor Robson when he urges that pension rights should accrue with each year of service, and have a definite surrender value. That is, after all, a system the value of which has been amply proved by university experience; and the Treasury itself has arranged interchangeability between the scientists and technologists it employs and the universities to and from which they frequently move by the simple expedient of making such officials part of the university superannuation scheme. I do not know how many people on the staffs of universities leave them for alternative careers; there are certainly faculties in which the loss is considerable. Maybe it ought to be far greater than it is; but it is at least far higher than in the upper classes of the Civil Service. And it is notable, compared with British methods, that Americans are here fantastically more experimental, and more willing to take risks, than is the case with ourselves. Of course Washington makes its mistakes, some of them bad mistakes. But at least it has never assumed, as Whitehall has overwhelmingly assumed, that you only look outside the service for the man you want in times of crisis like war; and expect him to leave when the crisis is over lest he interfere with the hopes aroused by seniority in the service. That is why appointments like that of Sir Henry Tizard, as the Government's Chief Scientific Adviser, or of Sir John Maud, as Permanent Secretary to the Minister of Education, give one some hope that, perhaps within a generation, one's sense of the apex of the administrative pyramid as very like a cathedral close will change to a comparison with the vivid and eager atmosphere that distinguished the Cavendish Laboratory, most notably in the days when Lord Rutherford was consul.

But I think mobility has a wider implication. Few things have impressed me more in the last fifteen years than the impact of that remarkable institution, the Imperial Defence College, upon the overseas officers who are seconded there. They do not merely bring a new atmosphere into the college itself; far more important, they take back to their own country on their return immensely wider horizons of thought, and also an exciting sense of possible new vistas. I think there would be immense gain if, year by year, we could send a reasonable number of young officials on exchange to an analogous department in a foreign government willing to accept such a system of exchange. I am thinking in terms beyond attendance on a Minister at an international conference or at Lake Success; there, of course, you are with your team which is doing its best to support the British Government's brief within the boundaries of which it must dwell. If a young Board of Trade official could spend a year in the Department of Commerce at Washington, or a Principal in the Home Office exchange with some-one in the American Department of Justice, I think there would be a chance of scrutinising traditional methods from a new angle which, after a few years, would begin by accumulation to have an important aspect. Could anything be better than the organisation by the Minister of Education of an annual interchange between one of his assistant inspectors and his opposite number in the French Ministry of Public Instruction? Would it not be invalu-able for one of Lord Citrine's young administrators to spend six months working as an official in the Tennessee Valley Authority? Or, taking a different basis, would it not be invaluable to take an official for three months every three or four years, at the period when his mind had not been adjusted to the historic routine of his De-partment, and send him abroad to report on the way in which one of its problems is solved elsewhere, with the condition attached that his report is not only to be com-pletely frank, but to explain, so far as he can, how what is meritorious in the foreign approach can be most usefully adapted to the situation here. I should, if I may venture to say so, feel far happier about the future of technological training in Great Britain if I were sure that a group of officials in the Ministry of Education had grasped at first hand the implications of the two great Institutes of Technology in Massachusetts and in California. For, compared to what they achieve, I am confident that the best we have in this area of training is a pretty shabby substitute.

There are two other points, arising from our experience since 1914, upon which I should like to touch. The first is my conviction, after nearly twenty-five years as a member of the Civil Service Arbitration Tribunal, that both in the clerical and in the executive grades, there is a very considerable amount of really first-class ability which our system of administration fails to discover, and therefore leaves only too often frustrated. That the change in post-entry training, and the wider examination opportunities for inter-grade promotions, have improved things since 1948 especially I should not deny for a moment; I should like, indeed, to pay my tribute to the enthusiasm the Director of Training, Mr. A. P. Sinker, in particular, has brought to his work. Yet, quite frankly, all that has been done reaches but a little way. Many of those whom I have in mind are not the type whom our normal or special methods of examination discover. What we need is more experiment in the Departments with young men and women who show signs of exceptional gifts. I remember one student of my own, then a clerical officer, who came to the London School of Economics and Political Science, got a First Class in his degree by evening work and got himself called to the Bar; no doubt all this was noted on his record, but nothing happened. I spoke about him to the late Sir Warren

Fisher, then Permanent Secretary of the Treasury, told him of the young man's anxiety to stay in the service, and urged Sir Warren to give him a chance of proving his quality in a higher grade. I know how hard Sir Warren knocked at many Departmental doors, and how disappointed he was when he found that none opened in reply. Meanwhile, my old student was offered a chance in the chambers of a very distinguished barrister. After nearly a year of waiting, he accepted the chance, and is now himself a distinguished King's Counsel with a large practice. While, of course, I do not for a moment deny that this was an exceptional case, it is one of the important tasks of the Civil Service to discover unused talent and open the door to it. I think it would repay this country many times over if it set aside some such sum as half a million pounds a year to spend on acting appointments to be offered to officials who show special promise in the lower grades. I do not doubt that there will be failures, some of them deeply disappointing failures; but if ten really first-rate people get their chance each year, I venture the view that the money will be well spent.

The last point I want to make in relation to the experience of the last generation concerns Treasury Control. I know and I admire the skill with which Treasury officials scale down the ardent optimism of the spending Departments. I agree that no plan ought ever to go before the Cabinet for approval until its financial aspects have been coldly and starkly examined under the auspices of the Chancellor of the Exchequer. I am aware that only the Service Departments can put their proposals before the Treasury with that sort of jaunty air which a pugilist wears when he expects to enter the ring at least on equal terms with his opponent. But I am convinced that it is a grave administrative mistake to concentrate this massive power of negation in the hands of, relatively, a small number of officials who have no other function but the forthright utterance of the Everlasting Nay. Treasury Control has three results. In the first place, it encourages a spending Department to ask for more than it wants, in the conviction that, when the Treasury axe has descended, it will have a sporting chance of being left with what it believes it really needs. In the second, the Treasury, unless overruled, will normally insist upon economies, in order to prove to the Chancellor that it is unceasingly vigilant upon his behalf. In the third, it gets officials who quickly are schooled to that habit of mind which views any economy as good in itself, without any effectively proportionate regard to the objectives against which the economies are directed. I should like to illustrate this by examples which, though small in themselves, illustrate the cheese-paring habit that is bred by centralising the power of negation in one branch, without other functions, of this historic organisation.

For many more years than I can remember, scholars beyond count have desired that the Reading Room and Library of the British Museum be opened in the evenings as well as in the daytime. The convenience of this to scholars who have other work in the day, and can thus make use of it only during their vacations, as well as to the *savant* from abroad who may have only a limited period in which, perhaps once in four or five years, to consult the remarkable wealth of material is too obvious to need

P

discussion. But the grant to the Museum has never been on a scale sufficient to persuade the trustees that the cost of keeping open in the evening would not involve them in other economies which they regard as less desirable. Nor does the Treasury Grant, whether direct, or through the appropriate Ministry, to any of our great national collections, whether of art, or science, or natural history, or of books, enable them to compete on equal terms in the acquisition of treasures which are either part of our own national heritage, or obviously worth buying for their own sake. And in books and manuscripts, there are great *lacunae* in the British Museum—rarely filled by the resources of other libraries in this country—which are due to the fact that the limitations within which the Museum must spend make it incapable of competing not merely with other great collections abroad, but also with individual collectors; and to this must be added the fact that their publications essential to scholars emerge so slowly, and are so prohibitive, as a rule, in price, that only a fairly small number of those who urgently require them can hope to afford them; in addition, great numbers of them are out of print and excessively scarce, though the prospect of reprinting them is, too often, beyond the resources of the governing body of any of the institutions concerned. Think of the pictures we have lost to the Morgans, the Mellons, the Fricks, or the books and manuscripts to the Morgans, the Huntingtons, the Folgers, and their like. On the Common Law before 1776, the Library of the Harvard Law School is far richer than the Museum, the Inns of Court, and the Law Society, when all their collections are put together. I admit gladly that the

Americans house them nobly, as in the Huntington and Folger Libraries, and not seldom put them to a use which shames us by its quality. But much of what American munificence has purchased for the United States belongs to the central stream of our cultural tradition, and it is a reflection on our pride in our own achievement that we should have been willing to let them go. The Chartist Movement, for example, is a vital aspect of British history in the nineteenth century. Its chief periodical is the *Northern Star*, and the only complete file of it was bought in the nineteen-twenties by the Marx-Engels Institute in Moscow. All our libraries are defective upon such matters as American history and institutions, and Russian history and institutions. One would have thought, for example, that if only because of our immense responsibilities in Africa and Malaya, our great library would have been careful to collect the laws, the decrees, the reports of anthropological expeditions, the accounts of methods by which, in a generation, many of the backward peoples in the Caucasus and the Arctic Circle have begun to conquer the tremendous problem of illiteracy, with all that this conquest means for economic development; in fact, hardly a fraction of this literature exists in any British Library, and no continuous effort was made to secure it even in the days before the "Cold War". Many of the most precious volumes of our own Rolls series are almost unobtainable, at any rate by those who live on an academic salary, and a large part of the invaluable Reports of the Historical Manuscripts Commission, and of the great Calendars of State Papers, are not likely again to be in a private library, unless of a fairly wealthy scholar. Even the reprint of the Catalogue of the British Museum is due to the generosity of the Rockefeller Foundation in New York and, whatever their goodwill, was far beyond the resources of the Museum's trustees.

I have made some enquiries from the specialists in these matters and they tell me that, given a grant of one million pounds annually for all the national collections—art, books, science, manuscripts and so on—which we need to keep our place in the stream of cultural development, all the main needs could be met; and it would be only very occasionally that some quite remarkable discovery would need exceptional assistance. One million pounds annually is one eight-hundredth part of what we are spending on armaments; it is one-tenth of what we spend when we build a medium-size aircraft carrier; it is barely one-fifth of what we spend on the Central Office of Information; it is less by a good deal than what it costs annually to run the Overseas Service of the B.B.C. Yet neither the remarkable success of the Arts Council, nor the revolution in musical taste that has been achieved by the endowment of a very small number of orchestras by Broadcasting House, has moved the Treasury to think of this area of activity in the very moderately generous terms I have suggested—its habit is to put economy first, and civilisation a fairly long way after. It is for this reason—an illustration only—that I would deprive the Treasury of the commanding authority of negation its centralised control now enables it normally to exercise. I accept at once the need for a body to make a financial case against any proposed expansion in expenditure, to show that it is wasteful, or undesirable, or badly timed;

and I accept also the probability that its long experience makes the Treasury about the best organ of government available to state that case. But, subject to an appeal by the Chancellor of the Exchequer to the Cabinet, I should prefer to see the provisional decision in the hands of a committee of high permanent officials, three perhaps, or five, whenever policy was involved outside routine matters, and wherever the cost of the proposal concerned was over a quarter of a million sterling, which should have the case for, as well as the case against, the proposal and report upon it to the Cabinet after an interval which allowed the Chancellor to make up his mind whether he would appeal against a defeat of the Treasury's case. I do not think the committee should always consist of the same members, because there is an obvious value in making the great civil servants look at problems beyond their own Departments as well as those inside them. The committee, I think, must be composed of officials, since it will be concerned with policy-making for which the Cabinet is ultimately responsible to Parliament; and a varying composition would prevent fellow-sufferers from the Treasury from continuing to get their revenge for the long years it has insisted on camels passing through the eye of a needle. But at least it would compel the Cabinet to realise that the Chancellor is often advised by men trained in the habit of being penny wise and pound foolish, who are inclined to insist that the man or the Department with a vision blot it out from his sight. That compulsion, in my submission, would be a day of creative liberation in the Civil Service of this country. For, if you take the period from somewhere round the time of Gladstone to

somewhere round the outbreak of the first World War,
I think it is true to say that the impact of Treasury control upon the national life has been to stunt the growth,
and limit the purposes of some of the major principles of
civilised living. If I may borrow an analogy from my
friend Mr. G. M. Young, I think the ugly drabness of
Swinton or Salford represents the character of Treasury
Control, while Marlborough and Salisbury represent
the cultivation of the standards the impact of which is to
elevate the dignity of our citizens. I am deeply concerned
that the second approach shall prevail.

XIII

THE POLITICAL RIGHTS AND SOCIAL INTERESTS
OF CIVIL SERVANTS

I turn to a very different issue—now a matter of acute
controversy—on which I think far more clear and frank
thought is necessary than it has thus far received—I mean
the degree to which we ought to place restrictions on the
political rights of civil servants. I should like to begin by
saying at once that the Report of the Masterman Committee seems to me a woeful and timid document, built
on a distrust of the honesty and loyalty of many hundred
thousand civil servants who have given many years'
proof that this distrust is utterly without justification. I
think it is absurd to insist that once a civil servant, not in
the industrial grades, becomes a candidate for Parliament
he shall resign his post. I think it is even more absurd to
lay it down that civil servants shall not play a part, in their

leisure time, in the political organisation in which they believe. Above all, I believe it is a great mistake to separate the vast majority of officials from work in local government where, very often, their experience of administration would enable them to make an important contribution to the standards of administration. I do not believe that the public would lose confidence in the detachment and loyalty of civil servants if, under agreed conventions, they were given the chance of exercising the rights of a citizen. And let me add that, in my judgment, the Masterman Committee was quite wrong in its view that the rules it laid down would, if the Government accepted them, give the public that assurance of neutrality that it would not have under conditions like those of the United States or of France. I was asked by the Committee if I disapproved the purposes of the Hatch Act in the American Civil Service. But the situation with which the Hatch Act was intended to deal had no relation to anything practised in this country for something like a century; its purpose was to prevent the Republican or the Democratic Parties from being able to levy a percentage tax on every civil servant they nominated to office to fill the party treasury at election times. In the French system a great many civil servants, of whom perhaps the best known among those living is that eminent humanist, M. Léon Blum, have played their part in politics without any deterioration in their work; and I have known scores of lesser cases in which the official's political affiliation was both active and known without producing the conviction that he would not be loyal to a Minister whose convictions were of a different school.

Let me begin by saying that officials do not need a special party connection in order to make their views obvious. No one, to my knowledge, ever thought of the Treasury as a nest of socialist singing birds, despite their neutrality and detachment. Men like Sir Nevile Henderson and Sir Ronald Lindsay, Sir Horace Wilson and Sir John Anderson—even before he abandoned an administrative for a political career—left very few people in doubt about their opinions. I do not suppose that anyone who worked with him thought that Sir Evelyn Murray represented the kind of left-wing socialism for which the late James Maxton stood. An important Permanent Secretary lived always, until his recent retirement, at the Conservative Club; not impossibly that gave some kind of clue to his opinions. No one who ever knew the late Lord Welby, of the Treasury, suspected him of an enthusiasm for a protective tariff. No one who has known Sir Richard Hopkins has ever left him with the conviction that he was an ardent advocate of Keynesian economics. It is, of course, true that there are many thousands of civil servants with no political convictions at all; away from their offices they are interested, like the late A. B. Walkley, in the theatre, or, like Austin Dobson, in *vers de société* and polite, sometimes even charming essays on the eighteenth century, or, like the late Sir T. L. Heath of the Treasury, in the all-absorbing excitement of early Greek mathematics. Perhaps I may summarise this by saying that when an official had strong political opinions he could not conceal them from any but the most stupid of Ministers for more than the first hour of their relationship; and the real question was, and is, granted those convictions, was he capable of looking at the Minister's views with detachment, and of helping him to apply them with the full energy of his mind? The answer is, sometimes yes, and sometimes no. Sir Austen Chamberlain, in his autobiography, tells an admirable story of the Permanent Secretary of the Post Office when he was Postmaster-General. They quarrelled violently over a decision Sir Austen proposed to make until at last he told his official that he had made up his mind that the decision stood. Thereupon, Sir Austen tells us, his Permanent Secretary said, "Well, Postmaster-General, if you want to make a damned fool of yourself, I cannot prevent you from doing so. But at least I can show you how to do it with the least possible damage to the country." That is what I mean by loyalty and detachment, and I think they are qualities quite distinct from political convictions and party preferences. Certainly I greatly prefer the honest avowal of outlook of which Sir Austen tells to the secret connections formed with the Ulster Tories by Sir Henry Wilson when he was D.M.O. at the War Office, or to the way in which too many members of Lord French's staff in 1914–15 supplied Colonel Repington, then of *The Times*, with secret information to be used to discredit the Asquith Government then in power. I have myself heard a British diplomat urge strongly a course of action on the Italian Prime Minister wholly different from the policy the Foreign Secretary had announced as the attitude of the British Government in the House of Commons. I was not impressed by his smiling explanation to me that he was, of course, speaking to Signor de Gasperi as a purely private person. That kind of duality is, in my submission, incompatible with the qualities required by the Civil Service.

I deeply dislike doing by unilateral regulation by the Treasury what can be done through agreed conventions of behaviour after proper discussion at the National Whitley Council. And I think most of those agreed conventions suggest themselves. First, it is clear that all members of the administrative class should impose upon themselves a self-denying ordinance in the political sphere. They ought to resign if they want to be candidates for Parliament. They ought not to make political speeches. They ought not to write books or articles on the immediate issues of political controversy. They are too near the centre of power to do any of these things. A Tory Minister would not feel he could rely upon an official at this level if he were, at the same time, a prospective Labour candidate who, from time to time, spoke out against the Government of which his Minister was a member; I hope the reverse proposition to this is true, though I am not quite sure. They have access to all kinds of private information. They often see the vital Cabinet papers. They could not speak in public political controversy without being deeply influenced by what they know; and much of what they know, both personal and impersonal, is information only accessible to them by reason of their proximity to the Minister and the Cabinet. In my judgment, therefore, no member of the administrative class ought to have political rights unless he leaves the Civil Service.

But below the administrative class, I do not think that rule should apply. It is enough if an official in the executive or the clerical class give an undertaking, whether he becomes a Parliamentary candidate or takes an active interest in his party, not to discuss in public the affairs of the Department to which he belongs, nor to reveal information which he obtains by virtue of his position in the service; if he were to break his undertaking the Permanent Secretary would be justified in recommending disciplinary action, though I should hope that, before the Permanent Secretary made his proposal to the Minister, he would discuss it with the Departmental Whitley Council and proceed, if possible, with its approval. I should give officials who became Parliamentary candidates leave, with pay, for the period of their election. If they were defeated, they would return to the Department in the ordinary way. If they were elected, I should put them on a special list, the officials on which would be free to return to the Department, if they were defeated in the next election, in their old grade, and with any increments of pay which had normally accrued to them; if, however, they were returned for a second Parliament, I should assume that this operated as a normal resignation from the service, though I should hope that they would receive a due proportion of the pension rights they would have received on retirement. I frankly see no difficulty in this. I do not really think such a candidature would embarrass the Department. And if it is a question of practical activity other than that of a candidate, I feel pretty certain that no Manchester constituency would be seriously concerned about the fairness of civil servants if, let us say, a woman shorthand typist in the area office of the Ministry of Health made a swingeing attack in the

Exchange division at a Tory meeting on the folly of Mr. Strachey's groundnuts scheme, or a clerical officer in the office of the local Inspector of Taxes spoke with some heat about the refusal of the Home Secretary to ban the Fascist Party. Assuming that the average civil servant observes the normal decencies of political behaviour, I am unable to believe that the liberation of the grades below the administrative would shock any public opinion or do any harm to the work of the Departments.

In the field of local government, different considerations arise. I do not think that an official of any rank in the area office of a Ministry should be a candidate for a local authority if his position gives him the chance of showing favouritism to the electorate from which he seeks votes. That seems to me to be true of National Insurance officials, local tax officers, the staffs of Labour Exchanges, and the officials concerned with rationing and the supplies of petrol. I doubt whether more than an occasional official would yield to the temptation to abuse his power in this way; but it is wholly right that no suspicion that the temptation is there should fall upon the Departments they represent. We must therefore draw an arbitrary line between officials in Departments of this type and other officials—clerks, for example, in the outstations of the War Office or members of the executive class in the local offices of the Ministry of Education. I see no reason why, candidatures apart, all civil servants below the Executive Grade should not be permitted to engage in political activity in local government matters, if they are so minded, provided always that they abstain from the use of any information which has come to them in the course of their official duties, and would not, otherwise, have been available to them. I sat for eleven years on a borough council in London on which there were five civil servants. They were guilty of no indiscretions. Their training enabled them to make a really valuable contribution to the council's work, and one of them, who was in an accounting branch of his Department, was of immense help on the council's finance committee. During all the eleven years I heard no murmur of disapproval from the electorate at their presence on the council. The Civil Service certainly did not suffer; and as we always sat in the evening, whether in full council or in committee, there was no need for any of them to ask for time off for the performance of their duties. I should agree that different considerations would arise if the local government body involved, like the London County Council, perhaps as much as three days of work each week in the daytime; the conflict, in such circumstances, between the claims of the Civil Service, which is the official's vocation, and the claims of the local body which he joins, it may be from the highest of civil motives, but nevertheless as a method, however admirable, of using his leisure, must be resolved by his recognition that his duty to the Civil Service comes first and that he cannot engage in any spare-time activities which prevent him from giving to his Department the time it requires from him.

There are two related questions upon which I should like to say a word. I hope we shall rapidly end the system which prohibits the civil servant from writing upon politics and public administration save by the permission of the Department. Here again my view is that there should be the right to freedom limited only by some obvious conventions which could easily be agreed through discussion in the Whitley organisation at national and departmental levels. I do not think an official of the Foreign Office should attack his Minister, or his Minister's policy, in an article or book; and, on the whole, I think it would be unwise for him to attack the defence policy, or its cost, which arises from that policy. But I thought it a serious injustice when, some twenty years ago, Sir Warren Fisher, then the Permanent Secretary of the Treasury, dismissed an official in the Ministry of Health for writing, under a pseudonym, an article which praised Mussolini's regime. I should be eager, generally speaking, to encourage civil servants, within the limits I have suggested, to write about the problems of politics and public administration without the sense of inhibition which now permeates most of what they are permitted to publish. If one examines the books civil servants write on their own Departments most of them suffer from a pretty devastating lack of vitality. Good examples of this are the volumes in the Whitehall series which are, mostly, about as interesting as an auctioneer's catalogue of the contents of a semi-detached house in a dormitory suburb; and even the occasional anecdote which is intended to make the books a little more lively is usually about some figure in the Department discussed who died anything from thirty to fifty years ago. Even the discussion of problems in the technique of administration stops, as a rule, at the point where significant generalisation could be made. Nobody has ever written on the practice of the Department a book as penetrating and as creative as the famous account of Parliamentary procedure which Sir Erskine May began, and so many of his successors have enriched and extended. There have been few examinations of the relation of a Department to the process of consultation with the public which can compare with the now classic analysis given by Sir Arthur Salter in his *Allied Shipping Control* a generation ago; and, when he wrote it, Sir Arthur had already left the Civil Service to become an official in the League of Nations. Lord Beveridge wrote an illuminating book on the Ministry of Food; but he had already ceased to have any official capacity when he wrote it. I welcome the remarkable volume in which Professor Hancock has inaugurated the history of civil administration in the second World War; but I do not think it is unjust to him to say that, broadly speaking, he describes the anatomy, rather than the physiology, of the processes which led to the planning of victory.

In all these cases, we are given some real insight into the processes of administration; but in all these cases the civil servant who writes them may fairly be said to have ceased to be a civil servant. I think it is an important thing for the powers that be to encourage officials within the widest possible limits that are reasonable to try to make explicit if not the "science" of public administration—it may well be that the logic of its relations lacks sufficient unity to permit it to be termed a "science"—at any rate the nature of public administration as an art. Not even the full and frank evidence often given by civil servants to Royal Commissions like that presided over by Lord MacDonnell in 1913–14, or that presided over by Lord Tomlin in 1930, really compensate for the absence of continuing discussion. Nor does the publication, by some Departments, of excellent pamphlets describing the character of their work, that of the Post Office, for example, or the account of the Department of Scientific and Industrial Research, really tell us what we want to know. Lord Chorley, for example, thinks that, while there are many notable exceptions, "on the whole there is a low level of personal vitality in the service" and he quotes with approval the criticisms of Sir Michael Sadler which I have cited elsewhere. Mr. H. R. G. Greaves, in an incisive analysis, has pointed out, on the basis of a considerable body of opinion between the two World Wars, that a "deterioration took place in the general level of vigour and imaginativeness of the administrator". Like Lord Chorley, Mr. Greaves admits there were exceptions, and "some continued to fight a losing and thankless battle", but he points out, quite fairly I think, that despite our knowledge of the anger and despair of a number of high officials at what they regarded as the disastrous policies of their political chiefs, "one of the most remarkable facts is that there were no resignations of high civil servants given in order to fight in independence for principles and policies in which they believed". That must be set in the context of the Report of the Committee on the Training of Civil Servants, published in 1944, which, while not agreeing that the faults alleged existed as widely as was complained, did admit that "over-devotion to precedent, lack of initiative and imagination . . . procrastination, and unwillingness to take responsibility or to give decisions" were important blemishes on the service.

Both in the new methods of admission to the service,

and in post-entry training, there is some evidence that the Civil Service Commission, and the Director of Training at the Treasury, are agreed that ability shown at an entrance examination in which there is a pretty clear advantage for the candidate who has taken the historic discipline of Oxford and of Cambridge is not enough to prove that the young official is likely to show equal ability in handling the problems of the Ministry of Health or of the Colonial Office—or to maintain a high standard of interest either in the administrative art itself or in the subject-matter with which he is set to deal. While I agree with Mr. Greaves that the situation ought to compel the recognition in the entrance examination itself that a comprehensive grasp of the social sciences ought to rank equally with the mastery of classical or mathematical studies, and that they should be central to all post-entry training, I believe that much the most important things are to broaden the area of recruitment to the administrative class, and to relax the present strictness of the rules against publication so that the official is encouraged to think about the problems with which he has to deal, and to embark upon research into them along his own line, instead of fitting them into the traditional policy of the Department. Most of the evidence we have certainly goes to show that, in the Foreign Office and the Diplomatic Service, for example, there are not many officials who could grasp with ease and sympathy the kind of issue a new Socialist Government in Poland or in Hungary has to solve, but several who could feel at home in the Warsaw of the Colonels' regime, or the Budapest of Admiral Horthy. When these rulers were overthrown, and gave

Q

place to men whose social origins and purpose were quite different, it is not in any way unjust to say that our representatives there, as well as those who gave them instructions from London, tended to think of the new governments as temporary abnormalities which would soon give place to their old masters; and many of them felt that it was disloyal to the friends they had made in the old society to show a real interest in the new, or to recognise, as has mostly been the case, that the new society was, in fact, history's judgment upon the old. In the long years between the wars, when Rakosi was the prisoner of a Nazi-orientated despotism, the Foreign Office did not concern itself about his fate; but the moment that Cardinal Mindszenty was put on trial for offences that were not only grave, but mostly substantiated by formidable evidence, the Foreign Office had an emotional crisis which persuaded it into the position of an uncalled-for counsel for the defence, long before it was aware of what the charges against the Cardinal were going to be. I thought myself that the charges against Petkov, which resulted in his judicial murder in 1948, were outrageous, and I was glad that, under the authority conceded to it in the Treaty with Bulgaria, the intervention on his behalf by the British Government was, despite its failure, a wholly justified protest; but I was sorry when a similar protest was not made by the Government when, but a year afterwards, Kostov was tried and executed on charges even more obviously untrue than those brought, no doubt with his connivance, against Petkov.

The truth, I venture to think, is the very important one that to understand the problems we have to deal with in policy-making we must know those problems from "within", if our final judgment upon them is to have any sort of insight and proportionality. It would be deeply interesting to know, for example, what friendships exist in the Civil Service, outside the office, between members of the administrative class, and members of the executive class, still more of the clerical. All of these relations may make a difference to the approved size of rooms in grant-aided housing, or to whether the bath is in the kitchen, or is in a separate room, or as to how far the bright boy at school, with younger children in the house, is not severely handicapped in his effort to reach the level upon which he can hope for a university scholarship. It is, I submit, a pretty startling thing that no Home Office official has ever made a contribution of importance to the study of penology or of criminology. With all the immense experience of the Ministry of Health, none of its officials has contributed anything of major importance to the enormous issues raised by the obvious need to reconstruct the areas of local government. I cannot imagine a better way of evoking genuine interest and the "vitality" which Lord Chorley found inadequate than by asking the young assistant-principal to try out his powers upon matters of this kind, and seeing the kind of criticism his work receives outside the service. The Department would not be bound by his conclusions; and it would do him a world of good to have to discover for himself a way of self-expression which could not be really adequate unless, in attempting it, he sought to make contact with the varieties of opinion it would be necessary for him to examine, and even to seek to satisfy in other aspects of his work.

All these questions, I must add, are further complicated by the large-scale growth of state-controlled industry, especially in the form of the Public Corporation. We have grown into the acceptance of the Public Corporation as the form that nationally owned industries should assume, less, I think, because everyone is agreed that this is their appropriate way of organisation than because business men have said, so long and so loudly, that you could not run an industry in national hands as the Post Office has been run for a century or so, that the business men's attitude has been taken for granted. We have thus three ranges of problem which require the most careful observation and analysis. There are the relations between the Minister and the National Board which directly governs the industry, as there are the relations between the National Board and the Regional Boards which the scale of these industries requires if they are not to be overloaded with detail at their summit. There are the internal staff relations, industrial and administrative, the methods of recruiting, promotion, training and so forth, and the external staff relations, the position of the Boards, for example, with respect to trade unions, or to the consumers, both domestic and foreign, of their produce. There is, further, the range of problems connected with the right of Parliament to be informed about the working of the nationalised industries, and the important question of how far Parliamentary questions can reach into the details of the industries' organisation and performance.

We have had, of course, a general spate of books about the Public Corporation, some good and some bad; we have had numerous debates in Parliament, papers before learned societies, a few deeply interesting reflections upon the questions to which they give rise, notably one from an eminent ex-civil servant now the deputy-chairman of a Public Corporation, Sir Arthur Street. Yet I do not think it can be said that we have reached a stage in these matters upon which any really acceptable generalisations can be laid down. I am not myself convinced that the Public Corporation has shown results so much better than those of the Post Office that it may be regarded as the general type which, with appropriate variations, will be the basis of all future nationalisation. I am far from persuaded that the recruitment of the National and Regional Boards is, so far, satisfactory; I am, for instance, very sceptical about the wisdom of taking a civil servant just on the verge of retirement, and making him the head of a National Board, with twice the salary he was receiving while he was a Permanent Secretary of a Department, over three times the pension he expected to obtain, and probably from seven to ten additional years in his career beyond what would have been open to him in the Civil Service. I doubt whether this kind of choice is likely to be good for morale in Whitehall. I am sceptical, too, about both the composition and the powers of the Regional Boards; and I am quite confident that no serious defence of the part-time member is possible. So far, I have not seen attempts at serious experiments in industrial democracy in any of the Public Corporations, and though I am inclined, from what I have seen, to believe that the temper of industrial relations is better, there is little that is really exciting in the relations between management and men. I should, on the whole, be prepared to agree that the Minister ought not to interfere with the daily running of a nationalised industry, and that, therefore, Parliamentary questions should be confined to matters of a fairly general nature; but I should also argue that, when any Public Corporation publishes its annual report, or when some important feature in its affairs comes to light, the House of Commons should have the means of enquiring into either, through an appropriate committee of its own, and that a general debate should only follow after that committee has reported back to the House the results of its investigations.

There are two other points in this field which seem to me to require emphasis. The first concerns the staffing of a nationalised industry. I think it is important that recruitment should not be done in a hole-and-corner way but by the public advertisement of vacancies, both local and national, with some kind of permanent machinery of inspection not wholly composed of men inside the industry, but with the kind of check which comes when a skilled outsider watches the choice, and performs that function long enough to have a real insight into its working. I am convinced, further, that there is a good deal to be said for reserving a number of administrative vacancies in any public enterprise for civil servants who shall enter them for a period of years to get the kind of practice in decision-making on the spot that a young official at the Colonial Office receives when he is sent off for a period on a tour of duty in the non-self-governing empire. This gives him a direct responsibility for decision-making—as distinct from the consideration of decisions proposed or already made—which is an important part of any properly conceived administrative experience. If I may use a very simple analogy, it is the difference between being a member of the public library committee of a local authority, with on the one hand little or no previous experience in satisfying the wants of those who use the library, and on the other, during one's membership, serving for a period behind the counter, so as to become really acquainted at first-hand with the infinite variety of needs which a librarian must seek to satisfy. To these, I add my third point that the tests of efficient operation in a nationalised industry cannot be, and ought not to be, the same as those for that industry when it was in private hands. Where the privately owned industry is concerned, the business of its directors is to make a profit for the shareholders; whatever else they do is incidental to that supreme end. A great company, for example, which, during the second World War, gave a handsome donation to Mrs. Churchill's Russian Fund, did so for the purposes of prestige; it was buying good-will which it hoped later to utilise for profit. But I can well conceive that a Government can take the attitude to a nationalised industry that the commodity it produces should be given rather than sold to the consumer, or sold to him at a below-cost rate, with the burden of the expenditure being carried by the taxpayer, or charged against the profits made in some other branch of nationalised industry. It might well prove to be desirable, for example, to persuade people to see the world at first-hand outside Great Britain so that they have the chance of overcoming the somewhat insular view that there is nothing like Blackpool; and were this view to be accepted low-cost air travel subsidised by the Exchequer, even though it made it impossible for B.O.A.C. to make a profit, might well be justified. If you have as great a belief as I have in the immense cultural value of travel abroad, and you are anxious to make the idea of holidays with pay something more than a week or a fortnight in not very comfortable rooms in, say, Margate or Whitley Bay, with the mother tied down by the neck to look after two or three young children, and the father mostly feeling that it is not very noble on his part to leave her to play the part of nurse-maid until it is the children's bedtime, when their sources of common enjoyment are usually limited to the movies, or a walk with a visit to the "local", or, it may be, a game of cards with their fellow-guests in the boarding house they have chosen, you may begin to think, as I do, that well-organised and cheap holiday camps for children, with a chance for the parents to go by air to Florence or to the Midi, or the Bernese Oberland, or, to be really daring, for a brief visit to Canada or to the United States, may be infinitely worth while, and as worth subsidising as the ballet, and not less likely to produce a valuable re-turn than the expenditure upon the British Council. The test of a nation's efficiency is, of course, the over-all ability at once to pay its way, and to see that its citizens have lives that are dignified and spacious. If we accept that test, we may then, in my judgment, deny that the criteria of effici-ency in a particular nationalised industry must be measured by financial standards only. It then follows that the habits of the business man's world must not dominate the new emerging social order; for it is emerging precisely in order that we may get away from the business man's world.

XIV

THE SCIENTIST IN THE CIVIL SERVICE

I turn, finally, to what I believe is going to be one of the outstanding problems of administration in this country for, given peace, something like the next two generations of its history. That problem is the place of the scientist in the Civil Service, his pay and conditions, his relation to the administrator and the politician, and the degree to which the Government should deliberately set out to create a fuller place for, and understanding of, science and technology in the national life. One thing, at least, is certain and agreed. Before 1939, the position was in every way unsatisfactory. Scientific civil servants were underpaid, their status in the bureaucratic hierarchy was both inadequate and indeterminate, their organisation was chaotic, and it was rare that the Government was able to retain the services of a really first-rate scientist or technologist against the competing claims of the universities and of industry. There were, in fact, before 1945, three important indices to the governmental attitude to the public significance of science. The first was the very small amount spent upon it, and the fact that, even of this small amount, by far the largest item was for research into the defence services. The second was the general failure of the politicians and of most of the heads of Departments to gauge the speed and volume of scientific advance, so that it was too often true that the men upon whom they depended for advice and action frequently belonged to a generation whose attitude had already been rendered obsolete by new developments. The third was the comparative failure to urge upon schools and universities, on the one hand, and upon manufacturers, on the other, the urgency of making the significance of science understood in their curricula and in their process of production respectively. It is hardly necessary for me to point out that by far the largest part of the nation's children do not even know what science means when they leave school, and that the university position was unsatisfactory both in relation to the number taking a first scientific degree, and in relation to the number engaged in advanced studies. The effort, moreover, made after 1919, to encourage industrial research by forming associations to which the Government made a grant in proportion to the subscriptions paid by firms in particular industries was not very successful; the great corporations, like Imperial Chemicals, preferred to do their own research without sharing its results with outside bodies, while few of the smaller firms knew how to utilise technological discoveries when these were communicated to them. The number was small, further, in all business categories which could appreciate the application of the social sciences to their own work; though it ought, in fairness, to be added that this absence of appreciation was characteristic of the Government as well.

It may be said without injustice that only when the second World War was well under way did the Government begin to realise the problems it confronted, grave enough in the struggle itself, but certain to be still more grave when victory was won. The White Paper on the future position of the scientist in the Civil Service, and the

Barlow Committee's *Report on Scientific Manpower*, were both admissions that the whole problem had to be looked at afresh. It was, perhaps, a pity that the Clapham Committee, which reported on the relations between the social sciences and the Government, reported in a sense which failed to realise either their importance in building up a quantitative basis for administration, or such an institutional connection between the specialist in the social sciences and the Government as to assure either the full endowment of research or the full utilisation of the social sciences by the Departments. It is, no doubt, true that there has never before been so much attention paid to the importance of science and the scientist in Whitehall as there is at the present time. But it still remains true that the attention given falls woefully short of the attention required. The statistics of the University Grants Committee make it obvious that nothing like the effort required is being made to supply the grave shortage in scientific manpower emphasised by the Barlow Committee. No serious steps have been taken to attract into the secondary schools science masters and mistresses who could begin to train, in the desirable numbers, those who would be willing to take up scientific or technological research. There are still not enough schools of technology, and none of the existing schools is of the level we ought to have, either in equipment or in personnel. There has not yet been an adequate effort to co-ordinate the different aspects of scientific research in such a way as to make them lead, on one side, up to the point where, through the Committees mostly under the Lord President of the Council, the Cabinet is made fully aware of needs and achievements and, on the other side, to the maintenance of a proper relation between science in the different Government Departments, and science outside, as in the universities, or in research institutes, and the present methods of making the results of research known at the circumference of industry.

Although the situation has considerably improved in medicine, in the physical and biological sciences, and in agriculture (which ought not to be left in a compartment separated from biology), it remains for us to deal with the social sciences in the same way. Though there exists, of course, the Central Statistical Office, the Economic Secretariat of the Cabinet, and the small Department of Economic Planning, under Sir Edwin Plowden, there is no body to provide a parallel coherency in this field; and, for the lack of it, a good deal of work that ought to be undertaken is simply not attempted because it has not been able to attract the interest of one or other of the private foundations; and this gap is the more glaring because, inevitably, the existing bodies in Whitehall are almost always concerned with immediate problems, and only rarely with issues of long-term range. It is obvious that planned research in fields like anthropology, law, economics, political science, psychology, does not now exist in this country, and that what we require is on a far bigger scale than any of the existing bodies can afford. It is also obvious that there is no serious attempt to organise adequate contacts with other countries for the exchange of information and personnel. The shadow of a dead tradition upon the Clapham Report gravely handicaps the full-scale use of existing knowledge in these fields as well as the effort to extend with the swiftness that is now possible the boundaries of that knowledge.

Were we to possess, under the aegis of the Lord President, a Central Committee for Scientific and Technological Research, under which the existing research bodies could work, and to which each of them could send their representatives, it would become possible for the Government to have an over-all view of the relations of science to national needs. No such over-all view is possible today; and the personnel used is often chosen at random, the investigations attempted are selected without any coherent investigation of the total choice, and there is no organic relation between government science in this country and that attempted elsewhere. All this grows more important every day, partly because the organisation of scientific research is so much more complex, the apparatus required so much more expensive, and the need for a real unity of relations between research by government, research by academic bodies, and research by industries, so much more important; and not the least vital aspect of this unity is the danger, which has consistently grown since the explosion of the first atomic bomb, that secrecy in science will, within a short rather than a long period, destroy that idea of free interchange of ideas in the international community of science which is indispensable to its proper development. The perspective of this free interchange is all the more important when, as in our own day, there is probably a keener sense of social responsibility among men and women engaged in research than at any time since the seventeenth century.

Apart from more adequate organisation, and a

determined effort by the Government to keep secrecy in science within the narrowest possible limits—the experience of American scientists ought to show how vital this is—there are three more issues raised by the relation between science and government to which attention must be drawn. The first is the relation between the administrator and the scientist. It is an exceedingly difficult question. Few of our permanent officials have, at the highest level, any serious training in science, or even a general knowledge of its frontiers; while the number of Ministers with the requisite insight is smaller still. Entrance into the administrative class is still so much the permanent preserve of the man or woman who has studied the humanities at the universities that the man who enters one of the scientific Departments of government by the very fact that he entered through that door almost automatically rules himself out of consideration for the highest administrative posts. Yet it is plain enough that a number of scientists have great administrative gifts—the power, for example, of imaginative organisation, the ability to know intelligence when they meet it, skill in stating a complex problem so that it is capable of being grasped by a layman who gives his mind to it. That was true of men like James Henry, the great organiser of the Smithsonian Institution at Washington, of Sir John Simon, who, if not the actual founder of the public health service in this country, is certainly among its pre-eminent figures. It was true of Lord Kelvin, as it is true today of men like the eminent American physicist, J. Robert Oppenheimer, or our own J. D. Cockcroft, or the remarkable German chemist, Fritz Haber. I do not think our system makes sure enough that the claims of the scientist reach the Minister with the directness and pungency that are so urgent. No doubt, an appointment like that of Sir Henry Tizard to be Chief Scientific Adviser to the Lord President goes some way to making an effective relation between the scientist and the politician. But I should like to be sure that our organisation makes it possible, first, for a look-out to be kept for the scientist who has administrative capacity in an exceptional degree, and, second, to place no barriers in the way of his chance to use that capacity in the highest posts in the Civil Service. Still more, I would like to be certain that the scientist whose plans are overruled by the administrative head of his Department should have the right to put his case directly to the Minister, and, if he be persuasive enough, to secure the Minister's assent to his ideas. I do not want to see the scientist encouraged to hope for the creation of a technocracy, in which he and his fellow-scientists are a master-class. But I suggest that a Minister of Defence, who is told by his Permanent Secretary that, despite the importunity of the scientists in the Department, the Board of Admiralty is anxious to have more battleships than air-craft-carriers, more cruisers than submarines, would do well to have a full and frank debate with all the relevant scientific personnel, with the Prime Minister in the chair at a special meeting of the Committee of Defence, before he makes any final decision.

The second point I want to make is that the probability is high of our finding that operational research, as used with such remarkable effect during the war, may well be relevant and important in the social sciences during the period of peace. The Social Survey has shown how valuable the results may be when operational research is applied to appropriate material; in things like choices in goods, preferences in clothes, in houses, and in similar matters, we know enough to make predictions with reasonable accuracy so that the planning of production reduces wastage to a minimum. Another example is the remarkable appendix contributed to Lord Beveridge's *Full Employment in a Free Society*, where, by the brilliant use of extrapolation, Mr. Kaldor has shown how policy may be framed in the light of material so handled that new possibilities of prediction are opened; and the well-known American strategic bombing survey is a technique which has obvious application over a much wider social field. There are new techniques of statistical sampling which we must apply to social questions with which government has to concern itself. We have much to learn about the selection of men and women for the right jobs by some of the methods of psychological assessment employed in the choice of men and women for the various forms of defence activity during the war. I should like here to record my own view that, after long years as a university teacher, I am satisfied that our normal methods of testing ability by the written examination, sometimes accompanied, as at Oxford, by an oral examination, are open, save at the very bottom and the very top, to a high percentage of error, largely due to the bias of the personal equation in the examiner. I am fairly confident, also, that a statistical examination of the causes of bankruptcy made by translating into statistical form the remarkable information collected by the Board of

Trade officials would tell us much of importance about the capital required to set up a business, the relation of turnover to profit, the kind of previous training normally required by the successful business man, and so on. We need studies in the effect of location upon business success, of the relation of crime to occupation, of the social costs of differentiating the districts in our towns by income, of the relation of the size of family and its income to educational opportunity. We could use operational research in the study of output in relation to factory conditions in ways which might well lead to important changes in economic organisation. I should myself greatly like to see worked out the degree to which the centralisation of banking in recent years, with its consequential limitation upon the powers of local managers, has been responsible for a good deal of the decay and backwardness in small towns, and even of the movement of industry towards London. These are, of course, examples only; the essential thing I want to suggest is that by a proper adaptation of operational research to the social sciences we could plan both legislation and administration upon a basis which relied far less on the flair of a brilliant civil servant, and far more on analysed ascertainable knowledge than is now possible. There are many grim cases where that flair has led to mistakes in policy of Himalayan proportions.

The final point I wish to make is the simple one that a good deal of the power of democracy to survive depends upon the awareness in its citizens of what science means and of the significant part it plays in our lives. Here, I believe, the Government needs to re-examine the whole of our educational system with a view to making it able

R

to create a living interest in science that is not confined to specialists who, in one way or another, will adopt it as a profession. It is not an inspiring fact to know that very few people have awareness of the history of science, or recognise that the poor Luddites of a century and a half ago have their equivalents in our own day, among managers as well as among men. It is pathetic to remember that most makers of patent medicines flourish because so large a proportion of our people know nothing of human nature. The specialist journals apart, there are not five newspapers in Great Britain in which one could find a clear and coherent account of some scientific discovery like penicillin. The press will tell us of the discoverer's habits, photograph his wife and children and house, tell us that he smokes a pipe and likes a game of golf on Sunday and the name of his favourite film, but they are highly unlikely to tell us anything about the discovery itself, because they assume from their own lack of interest in it that we are uninterested too. Sir Oliver Lodge must have had a thousand times more publicity for his interest in communication with the dead than he ever received for his notable contributions to the physics of telecommunication. Much of our future will depend upon our ability to become aware of science. We must use all the instrumentalities at our disposal to make this awareness a natural part of our daily lives. For this is the one way to adapt ourselves to the claims of a swiftly changing world with the ease that comes from a grasp of why the claims make one road the road to life, and the other the road to death. This is an urgent matter, too urgent to be left to chance and voluntary effort. It is one of the keys to national survival. It was the realisation of its importance which led Plato to insist that the Minister of Education is more important than the Minister for War. I hope we shall all of us live long enough to see his affirmation fulfilled in time to prevent the wholesale destruction of civilised values. I hope that no Government assumes that it can examine this issue as though it had at its disposal the spacious chronology of the geologist. We are concerned with the short run, and not the long; for, as Keynes said in perhaps the best of all his aphorisms, in the long run we shall all be dead.

INDEX